MznLnx

Missing Links Exam Preps

Exam Prep for

Management: Meeting and Exceeding Customer Expectations

Plunkett, Attner, & Allen, 8th Edition

The MznLnx Exam Prep is your link from the texbook and lecture to your exams.
The MznLnx Exam Preps are unauthorized and comprehensive reviews of your textbooks.

All material provided by MznLnx and Rico Publications (c) 2010
Textbook publishers and textbook authors do not particpate in or contribute to these reviews.

MznLnx

Rico Publications

Exam Prep for Management: Meeting and Exceeding Customer Expectations
8th Edition
Plunkett, Attner, & Allen

Publisher: Raymond Houge
Assistant Editor: Michael Rouger
Text and Cover Designer: Lisa Buckner
Marketing Manager: Sara Swagger
Project Manager, Editorial Production: Jerry Emerson
Art Director: Vernon Lowerui

Product Manager: Dave Mason
Editorial Assitant: Rachel Guzmanji
Pedagogy: Debra Long
Cover Image: Jim Reed/Getty Images
Text and Cover Printer: City Printing, Inc.
Compositor: Media Mix, Inc.

(c) 2010 Rico Publications

ALL RIGHTS RESERVED. No part of this work covered by the copyright may be reproduced or used in any form or by an means--graphic, electronic, or mechanical, including photocopying, recording, taping, Web distribution, information storage, and retrieval systems, or in any other manner--without the written permission of the publisher.

Printed in the United States
ISBN:

For more information about our products, contact us at:
Dave.Mason@RicoPublications.com

For permission to use material from this text or product, submit a request online to:
Dave.Mason@RicoPublications.com

Contents

CHAPTER 1
Management: An Overview — 1

CHAPTER 2
Management Thought: Past and Present — 8

CHAPTER 3
Management Ethics and Social Responsibility — 19

CHAPTER 4
Management`s Commitment to Quality and Productivity — 25

CHAPTER 5
The Manager`s Environment — 34

CHAPTER 6
Organizational Planning — 42

CHAPTER 7
Strategic Planning and Strategic Management — 47

CHAPTER 8
Making Decisions — 55

CHAPTER 9
Organizing Principles — 63

CHAPTER 10
Organizational Design — 72

CHAPTER 11
Organizational Structure and Change — 76

CHAPTER 12
Staffing — 88

CHAPTER 13
Communication: Interpersonal and Organizational — 102

CHAPTER 14
Human Motivation — 108

CHAPTER 15
Leadership — 118

CHAPTER 16
Team Management and Conflict — 122

CHAPTER 17
Information Management Systems — 128

CHAPTER 18
Controlling: Purpose and Process — 134

CHAPTER 19
Control Techniques — 140

CHAPTER 20
International Management — 148

Contents (Cont.)

CHAPTER 21
   Succeeding In Your Organization   151
ANSWER KEY   158

TO THE STUDENT

COMPREHENSIVE

The *MznLnx* Exam Prep series is designed to help you pass your exams. Editors at MznLnx review your textbooks and then prepare these practice exams to help you master the textbook material. Unlike study guides, workbooks, and practice tests provided by the texbook publisher and textbook authors, *MznLnx* gives you **all** of the material in each chapter in exam form, not just samples, so you can be sure to nail your exam.

MECHANICAL

The MznLnx Exam Prep series creates exams that will help you learn the subject matter as well as test you on your understanding. Each question is designed to help you master the concept. Just working through the exams, you gain an understanding of the subject--its a simple mechanical process that produces success.

INTEGRATED STUDY GUIDE AND REVIEW

MznLnx is not just a set of exams designed to test you, its also a comprehensive review of the subject content. Each exam question is also a review of the concept, making sure that you will get the answer correct without having to go to other sources of material. You learn as you go! Its the easiest way to pass an exam.

HUMOR

Studying can be tedious and dry. MznLnx's instructional design includes moderate humor within the exam questions on occassion, to break the tedium and revitalize the brain

Chapter 1. Management: An Overview

1. _____ was a writer, management consultant, and self-described 'social ecologist.' Widely considered to be 'the father of modern management,' his 39 books and countless scholarly and popular articles explored how humans are organized across all sectors of society--in business, government and the nonprofit world. His writings have predicted many of the major developments of the late twentieth century, including privatization and decentralization; the rise of Japan to economic world power; the decisive importance of marketing; and the emergence of the information society with its necessity of lifelong learning. In 1959, Drucker coined the term 'knowledge worker' and later in his life considered knowledge work productivity to be the next frontier of management.

   a. Chrissie Hynde
   b. Debora L. Spar
   c. Jacques Al-Salawat Nasruddin Nasser
   d. Peter Ferdinand Drucker

2. _____ is a term used in general business practice to describe methodologies, systems, and practices designed to generate new potential business clientele, generally operated through a variety of marketing techniques. _____ facilitates a business's connection between its outgoing consumer advertising and the responses to that advertising. These processes are designed for business-to-business and direct-to-consumer strategies.

   a. 1990 Clean Air Act
   b. Request for Proposal
   c. Lead generation
   d. Lead Management

3. _____ refers to both the industry of, and the practice of, helping organizations improve their performance, primarily through the analysis of existing business problems and development of plans for improvement.

   Organizations hire the services of management consultants for a number of reasons, including gaining external (and presumably objective) advice, access to the consultants' specialized expertise, or simply as extra temporary help during a one-time project, where the hiring of more permanent employees is not required.

   Because of their exposure to and relationships with numerous organizations, consultancies are also said to be aware of industry 'best practices', although the transferability of such practices from one organization to another is the subject of debate.

   a. 33 Strategies of War
   b. 1990 Clean Air Act
   c. Management Consulting
   d. 28-hour day

4. _____ in its literal sense is the process of transformation of local or regional phenomena into global ones. It can be described as a process by which the people of the world are unified into a single society and function together.

   This process is a combination of economic, technological, sociocultural and political forces.

   a. Collaborative Planning, Forecasting and Replenishment
   b. Cost Management
   c. Histogram
   d. Globalization

5. _____ is the process of recruiting individuals to fill executive positions in organizations. _____ may be performed by an organization's board of directors, by executives in the organization, or by an outside _____ organization.

   The _____ profession has two distinct fields, retained _____ and contingency search.

Chapter 1. Management: An Overview

a. Executive Search
c. Internet recruiting
b. Employment agency
d. Employee referral

6. _____ is a technical term used in management science popularized by Joseph M. Juran

He defined an internal and external customers as anyone affected by the product or by the process used to produce the product, in the context of quality management. _____s may play the role as supplier, processer, and customer in the sequence of product development.

He claimed that the organization must understand and identify both internal and external customers and their needs.

a. AAAI
c. A4e
b. A Stake in the Outcome
d. Internal customer

7. _____ has been described as the 'process of social influence in which one person can enlist the aid and support of others in the accomplishment of a common task' . A definition more inclusive of followers comes from Alan Keith of Genentech who said '_____ is ultimately about creating a way for people to contribute to making something extraordinary happen.'

_____ is one of the most salient aspects of the organizational context. However, defining _____ has been challenging.

a. 28-hour day
c. Situational leadership
b. 1990 Clean Air Act
d. Leadership

8. _____ consists of the processes a company uses to track and organize its contacts with its current and prospective customers. _____ software is used to support these processes; information about customers and customer interactions can be entered, stored and accessed by employees in different company departments. Typical _____ goals are to improve services provided to customers, and to use customer contact information for targeted marketing.

a. Green marketing
c. Marketing plan
b. Disruptive technology
d. Customer relationship management

9. The _____ is an independent agency of the United States government, established in 1914 by the _____ Act. Its principal mission is the promotion of 'consumer protection' and the elimination and prevention of what regulators perceive to be harmfully 'anti-competitive' business practices, such as coercive monopoly.

The _____ Act was one of President Wilson's major acts against trusts.

a. 1990 Clean Air Act
c. 28-hour day
b. 33 Strategies of War
d. Federal Trade Commission

10. _____ is a method of direct marketing in which a salesperson solicits to prospective customers to buy products or services, either over the phone or through a subsequent face to face or Web conferencing appointment scheduled during the call.

_____ can also include recorded sales pitches programmed to be played over the phone via automatic dialing. _____ has come under fire in recent years, being viewed as an annoyance by many.

   a. 1990 Clean Air Act   b. Telemarketing
   c. 33 Strategies of War   d. 28-hour day

11. The _____ is a Cabinet department of the United States government responsible for occupational safety, wage and hour standards, unemployment insurance benefits, re-employment services, and some economic statistics. Many U.S. states also have such departments. The department is headed by the United States Secretary of Labor.

   a. A Stake in the Outcome   b. United States Department of Labor
   c. AAAI   d. A4e

12. The 'business case for _____', theorizes that in a global marketplace, a company that employs a diverse workforce (both men and women, people of many generations, people from ethnically and racially diverse backgrounds etc.) is better able to understand the demographics of the marketplace it serves and is thus better equipped to thrive in that marketplace than a company that has a more limited range of employee demographics.

An additional corollary suggests that a company that supports the _____ of its workforce can also improve employee satisfaction, productivity and retention.

   a. Virtual team   b. Diversity
   c. Kanban   d. Trademark

13. In economics, business, retail, and accounting, a _____ is the value of money that has been used up to produce something, and hence is not available for use anymore. In economics, a _____ is an alternative that is given up as a result of a decision. In business, the _____ may be one of acquisition, in which case the amount of money expended to acquire it is counted as _____.

   a. Fixed costs   b. Cost overrun
   c. Cost allocation   d. Cost

14. _____ is the state or fact of exclusive rights and control over property, which may be an object, land/real estate or intellectual property. An _____ right is also referred to as title. The concept of _____ has existed for thousands of years and in all cultures.

   a. A Stake in the Outcome   b. Emanation of the state
   c. Ownership   d. A4e

15. _____ is unwelcome harassment of a sexual nature, or based upon the receiving party's sex or gender. In some contexts or circumstances, _____ may be illegal. It includes a range of behavior from seemingly mild transgressions and annoyances to actual sexual abuse or sexual assault.

   a. Hypernorms   b. 1990 Clean Air Act
   c. 28-hour day   d. Sexual Harassment

16. In economics, and cost accounting, _____ describes the total economic cost of production and is made up of variable costs, which vary according to the quantity of a good produced and include inputs such as labor and raw materials, plus fixed costs, which are independent of the quantity of a good produced and include inputs (capital) that cannot be varied in the short term, such as buildings and machinery. _____ in economics includes the total opportunity cost of each factor of production in addition to fixed and variable costs.

The rate at which _____ changes as the amount produced changes is called marginal cost.

a. Total Cost
b. 33 Strategies of War
c. 1990 Clean Air Act
d. 28-hour day

17. _____ is a financial estimate designed to help consumers and enterprise managers assess direct and indirect costs It is a form of full cost accounting.

a. Total Cost of Ownership
b. 33 Strategies of War
c. 1990 Clean Air Act
d. 28-hour day

18. _____ is a contract between two parties, one being the employer and the other being the employee. An employee may be defined as: 'A person in the service of another under any contract of hire, express or implied, oral or written, where the employer has the power or right to control and direct the employee in the material details of how the work is to be performed.' Black's Law Dictionary page 471 (5th ed. 1979.)

a. Employment rate
b. Employment counsellor
c. Employment
d. Exit interview

19. The term _____ was created by President Lyndon B. Johnson when he signed Executive Order 11246 on September 24, 1965, created to prohibit federal contractors from discriminating against employees on the basis of race, sex, creed, religion, color, or national origin. In more recent times, most employers have also added sexual orientation to the list of non-discrimination.

The Executive Order also required contractors to implement affirmative action plans to increase the participation of minorities and women in the workplace.

a. AAAI
b. A4e
c. A Stake in the Outcome
d. Equal employment opportunity

20. Organizational culture is not the same as _____. It is wider and deeper concepts, something that an organization 'is' rather than what it 'has' (according to Buchanan and Huczynski.)

_____ is the total sum of the values, customs, traditions and meanings that make a company unique.

a. Job analysis
b. Corporate Culture
c. Work design
d. Path-goal theory

Chapter 1. Management: An Overview

21. A _____ is a type of business entity in which partners (owners) share with each other the profits or losses of the business. _____s are often favored over corporations for taxation purposes, as the _____ structure does not generally incur a tax on profits before it is distributed to the partners (i.e. there is no dividend tax levied.) However, depending on the _____ structure and the jurisdiction in which it operates, owners of a _____ may be exposed to greater personal liability than they would as shareholders of a corporation.

   a. Mediation
   b. Due process
   c. Federal Employers Liability Act
   d. Partnership

22. A _____ also known as a sole trader, or simply proprietorship is a type of business entity which there is only one owner and he has the final word taking all desicions by himself. All debts of the business are debts of the owner and must pay from his personal possessions. This means that the owner has unlimited liabilty.

   a. Business rule
   b. Golden hello
   c. Sole proprietorship
   d. Foreign ownership

23. _____ is an increasingly broadening term with which an organization, or other human system describes the combination of traditionally administrative personnel functions with acquisition and application of skills, knowledge and experience, Employee Relations and resource planning at various levels. The field draws upon concepts developed in Industrial/Organizational Psychology and System Theory. _____ has at least two related interpretations depending on context. The original usage derives from political economy and economics, where it was traditionally called labor, one of four factors of production although this perspective is changing as a function of new and ongoing research into more strategic approaches at national levels. This first usage is used more in terms of '_____ development', and can go beyond just organizations to the level of nations. The more traditional usage within corporations and businesses refers to the individuals within a firm or agency, and to the portion of the organization that deals with hiring, firing, training, and other personnel issues, typically referred to as `_____ management'.

   a. Human resources
   b. Human resource management
   c. Progressive discipline
   d. Bradford Factor

24. _____ is an integrated communications-based process through which individuals and communities discover that existing and newly-identified needs and wants may be satisfied by the products and services of others.

_____ is defined by the American _____ Association as the activity, set of institutions, and processes for creating, communicating, delivering, and exchanging offerings that have value for customers, clients, partners, and society at large. The term developed from the original meaning which referred literally to going to market, as in shopping, or going to a market to buy or sell goods or services.

   a. Market development
   b. Marketing
   c. Customer relationship management
   d. Disruptive technology

25. _____ is a layer of management in an organization whose primary job responsibility is to monitor activities of subordinates while reporting to upper management.

In pre-computer times, _____ would collect information from junior management and reassemble it for senior management. With the advent of inexpensive PCs this function has been taken over by e-business systems.

a. Community management
c. Theory Y
b. Continuous monitoring
d. Middle management

26. _____ for short is a descriptive term for certain executives in a business operation. It is also a formal title held by some business executives, most commonly in the hospitality industry.

A _____ has broad, overall responsibility for a business or organization. Whereas a manager may be responsible for one functional area, the _____ is responsible for all areas.

a. Managing director
c. Chief technology officer
b. Chief knowledge officer
d. General manager

27. A _____ is a list of the general tasks and responsibilities of a position. Typically, it also includes to whom the position reports, specifications such as the qualifications needed by the person in the job, salary range for the position, etc. A _____ is usually developed by conducting a job analysis, which includes examining the tasks and sequences of tasks necessary to perform the job.

a. Recruitment Process Insourcing
c. Recruitment advertising
b. Job description
d. Recruitment

28. _____ is one of the managerial functions like planning, organizing, staffing and directing. It is an important function because it helps to check the errors and to take the corrective action so that deviation from standards are minimized and stated goals of the organization are achieved in desired manner. According to modern concepts, _____ is a foreseeing action whereas earlier concept of _____ was used only when errors were detected. _____ in management means setting standards, measuring actual performance and taking corrective action.

a. Schedule of reinforcement
c. Control
b. Turnover
d. Decision tree pruning

29. In politics, a _____, (by metaphor with the carved _____ at the prow of a sailing ship), is a person who holds an important title or office yet executes little actual power, most commonly limited by convention rather than law. Common _____s include constitutional monarchs, such as: Queen Elizabeth II, the Emperor of Japan, or presidents in parliamentary democracies, such as the President of Israel.

While the authority of a _____ is in practice generally symbolic, public opinion, respect for the office or the office holder and access to high levels of government can give them significant influence on events.

a. 33 Strategies of War
c. 1990 Clean Air Act
b. 28-hour day
d. Figurehead

30. An _____ is a person who has possession of an enterprise and assumes significant accountability for the inherent risks and the outcome. It is an ambitious leader who combines land, labor, and capital to create and market new goods or services. The term is a loanword from French and was first defined by the Irish economist Richard Cantillon.

a. A4e
c. AAAI
b. A Stake in the Outcome
d. Entrepreneur

31. In economics, _____ is the desire to own something and the ability to pay for it. The term _____ signifies the ability or the willingness to buy a particular commodity at a given point of time.

a. 1990 Clean Air Act
b. 28-hour day
c. Demand
d. 33 Strategies of War

32. _____ Movement refers to those researchers of organizational development who study the behavior of people in groups, in particular workplace groups. It originated in the 1920s' Hawthorne studies, which examined the effects of social relations, motivation and employee satisfaction on factory productivity. The movement viewed workers in terms of their psychology and fit with companies, rather than as interchangeable parts.
   a. Hersey-Blanchard situational theory
   b. Participatory management
   c. Work design
   d. Human relations

33. _____ is a recursive process where two or more people or organizations work together in an intersection of common goals -- for example, an intellectual endeavor that is creative in nature--by sharing knowledge, learning and building consensus. _____ does not require leadership and can sometimes bring better results through decentralization and egalitarianism. In particular, teams that work collaboratively can obtain greater resources, recognition and reward when facing competition for finite resources._____ is also present in opposing goals exhibiting the notion of adversarial _____, though this is not a common case for using the term.
   a. 1990 Clean Air Act
   b. 28-hour day
   c. Collaboration
   d. Collectivism

Chapter 2. Management Thought: Past and Present

1. Procter is a surname, and may also refer to:

   - Bryan Waller Procter (pseud. Barry Cornwall), English poet
   - Goodwin Procter, American law firm
   - _____, consumer products multinational

   a. Downstream
   b. Master and Servant Acts
   c. Strict liability
   d. Procter ' Gamble

2. _____ is a Fortune 500, American multinational corporation headquartered in Cincinnati, Ohio, that manufactures a wide range of consumer goods. As of 2008, P'G is the 8th largest corporation in the world by market capitalization and 14th largest US company by profit.
   a. Turnover
   b. Procter ' Gamble Co.
   c. Maturity of Organizations and Business Excellence - The Four-Phase Model
   d. STAR

3. A _____ is the term given to a company that facilitates the learning of its members and continuously transforms itself. _____s develop as a result of the pressures facing modern organizations and enables them to remain competitive in the business environment. A _____ has five main features; systems thinking, personal mastery, mental models, shared vision and team learning.
   a. 1990 Clean Air Act
   b. Hoshin Kanri
   c. Quality function deployment
   d. Learning organization

4. The _____ was a period in the late 18th and early 19th centuries when major changes in agriculture, manufacturing, mining, and transportation had a profound effect on the socioeconomic and cultural conditions in Britain. The changes subsequently spread throughout Europe, North America, and eventually the world. The onset of the _____ marked a major turning point in human society; almost every aspect of daily life was eventually influenced in some way.
   a. Abraham Harold Maslow
   b. Industrial Revolution
   c. Affiliation
   d. Adam Smith

5. The _____ is a United States statute that was passed in response to a series of United States Supreme Court decisions which limited the rights of employees who had sued their employers for discrimination. The Act represented the first effort since the passage of the Civil Rights Act of 1964 to modify some of the basic procedural and substantive rights provided by federal law in employment discrimination cases. It provided for the right to trial by jury on discrimination claims and introduced the possibility of emotional distress damages, while limiting the amount that a jury could award

   The 1991 Act combined elements from two different civil rights acts of the past: the Civil Rights Act of 1866, better known by the number assigned to it in the codification of federal laws as 'Section 1981', and the employment-related provisions of the Civil Rights Act of 1964, generally referred to as 'Title VII', its location within the Act.

   a. Covenant
   b. Civil Rights Act of 1991
   c. Negligence in employment
   d. Resource Conservation and Recovery Act

Chapter 2. Management Thought: Past and Present

6. A _____ is a type of bar chart that illustrates a project schedule. _____s illustrate the start and finish dates of the terminal elements and summary elements of a project. Terminal elements and summary elements comprise the work breakdown structure of the project.
   a. Gantt chart
   b. 1990 Clean Air Act
   c. 33 Strategies of War
   d. 28-hour day

7. The _____ is a monograph published by Frederick Winslow Taylor in 1911. This influential monograph is the basis of modern organization and decision theory and has motivated administrators and students of managerial technique. Taylor was an American mechanical engineer and a management consultant in his later years.
   a. 28-hour day
   b. 33 Strategies of War
   c. 1990 Clean Air Act
   d. Principles of Scientific Management

8. _____ is a theory of management that analyzes and synthesizes workflows, with the objective of improving labour productivity. The core ideas of the theory were developed by Frederick Winslow Taylor in the 1880s and 1890s, and were first published in his monographs, Shop Management and The Principles of _____ Taylor believed that decisions based upon tradition and rules of thumb should be replaced by precise procedures developed after careful study of an individual at work.
   a. Value engineering
   b. Scientific Management
   c. Master production schedule
   d. Capacity planning

9. _____, widely known as F. W. Taylor, was an American mechanical engineer who sought to improve industrial efficiency. He is regarded as the father of scientific management, and was one of the first management consultants.

Taylor was one of the intellectual leaders of the Efficiency Movement and his ideas, broadly conceived, were highly influential in the Progressive Era.

   a. Jonah Jacob Goldberg
   b. Frederick Winslow Taylor
   c. Geoffrey Colvin
   d. Douglas N. Daft

10. _____ is Latin for 'Let the buyer beware'. Generally _____ is the property law doctrine that controls the sale of real property after the date of closing.

Under the doctrine of _____, the buyer could not recover from the seller for defects on the property that rendered the property unfit for ordinary purposes. The only exception was if the seller actively concealed latent defects. The modern trend in the US, however, is one of the Implied Warranty of Fitness that applies only to the sale of new residential housing by a builder-seller and the rule of _____ applies to all other sale situations.

   a. 33 Strategies of War
   b. 1990 Clean Air Act
   c. 28-hour day
   d. Caveat emptor

11. _____ is a layer of management in an organization whose primary job responsibility is to monitor activities of subordinates while reporting to upper management.

In pre-computer times, _____ would collect information from junior management and reassemble it for senior management. With the advent of inexpensive PCs this function has been taken over by e-business systems.

Chapter 2. Management Thought: Past and Present

a. Community management
b. Theory Y
c. Continuous monitoring
d. Middle management

12. The _____ was a landmark piece of legislation in the United States that outlawed racial segregation in schools, public places, and employment.
a. Financial Security Law of France
b. Design patent
c. Negligence in employment
d. Civil Rights Act of 1964

13. _____ is one of the managerial functions like planning, organizing, staffing and directing. It is an important function because it helps to check the errors and to take the corrective action so that deviation from standards are minimized and stated goals of the organization are achieved in desired manner. According to modern concepts, _____ is a foreseeing action whereas earlier concept of _____ was used only when errors were detected. _____ in management means setting standards, measuring actual performance and taking corrective action.
a. Decision tree pruning
b. Schedule of reinforcement
c. Control
d. Turnover

14. _____ has been described as the 'process of social influence in which one person can enlist the aid and support of others in the accomplishment of a common task'. A definition more inclusive of followers comes from Alan Keith of Genentech who said '_____ is ultimately about creating a way for people to contribute to making something extraordinary happen.'

_____ is one of the most salient aspects of the organizational context. However, defining _____ has been challenging.

a. 1990 Clean Air Act
b. 28-hour day
c. Situational leadership
d. Leadership

15. _____ is unwelcome harassment of a sexual nature, or based upon the receiving party's sex or gender. In some contexts or circumstances, _____ may be illegal. It includes a range of behavior from seemingly mild transgressions and annoyances to actual sexual abuse or sexual assault.
a. 28-hour day
b. 1990 Clean Air Act
c. Hypernorms
d. Sexual Harassment

16. The 'business case for _____', theorizes that in a global marketplace, a company that employs a diverse workforce (both men and women, people of many generations, people from ethnically and racially diverse backgrounds etc.) is better able to understand the demographics of the marketplace it serves and is thus better equipped to thrive in that marketplace than a company that has a more limited range of employee demographics.

An additional corollary suggests that a company that supports the _____ of its workforce can also improve employee satisfaction, productivity and retention.

a. Kanban
b. Virtual team
c. Trademark
d. Diversity

17. _____ is a contract between two parties, one being the employer and the other being the employee. An employee may be defined as: 'A person in the service of another under any contract of hire, express or implied, oral or written, where the employer has the power or right to control and direct the employee in the material details of how the work is to be performed.' Black's Law Dictionary page 471 (5th ed. 1979.)

   a. Exit interview   b. Employment counsellor
   c. Employment rate   d. Employment

18. The term _____ was created by President Lyndon B. Johnson when he signed Executive Order 11246 on September 24, 1965, created to prohibit federal contractors from discriminating against employees on the basis of race, sex, creed, religion, color, or national origin. In more recent times, most employers have also added sexual orientation to the list of non-discrimination.

The Executive Order also required contractors to implement affirmative action plans to increase the participation of minorities and women in the workplace.

   a. A4e   b. Equal employment opportunity
   c. A Stake in the Outcome   d. AAAI

19. A _____ is a list of the general tasks and responsibilities of a position. Typically, it also includes to whom the position reports, specifications such as the qualifications needed by the person in the job, salary range for the position, etc. A _____ is usually developed by conducting a job analysis, which includes examining the tasks and sequences of tasks necessary to perform the job.

   a. Recruitment Process Insourcing   b. Recruitment
   c. Job description   d. Recruitment advertising

20. _____ is an advertisement in which a particular product specifically mentions a competitor by name for the express purpose of showing why the competitor is inferior to the product naming it.

This should not be confused with parody advertisements, where a fictional product is being advertised for the purpose of poking fun at the particular advertisement, nor should it be confused with the use of a coined brand name for the purpose of comparing the product without actually naming an actual competitor. ('Wikipedia tastes better and is less filling than the Encyclopedia Galactica.')

In the 1980s, during what has been referred to as the cola wars, soft-drink manufacturer Pepsi ran a series of advertisements where people, caught on hidden camera, in a blind taste test, chose Pepsi over rival Coca-Cola.

   a. 1990 Clean Air Act   b. 28-hour day
   c. 33 Strategies of War   d. Comparative advertising

21. _____ and Theory Y are theories of human motivation created and developed by Douglas McGregor at the MIT Sloan School of Management in the 1960s that have been used in human resource management, organizational behavior, organizational communication and organizational development. They describe two very different attitudes toward workforce motivation. McGregor felt that companies followed either one or the other approach.

In _____, which many managers practice, management assumes employees are inherently lazy and will avoid work if they can. They inherently dislike work. Because of this, workers need to be closely supervised and comprehensive systems of controls developed.

    a. Management team
    b. Cash cow
    c. Theory X
    d. Job enrichment

22. Theory X and _____ are theories of human motivation created and developed by Douglas McGregor at the MIT Sloan School of Management in the 1960s that have been used in human resource management, organizational behavior, organizational communication and organizational development. They describe two very different attitudes toward workforce motivation. McGregor felt that companies followed either one or the other approach.

In _____, management assumes employees may be ambitious and self-motivated and exercise self-control. It is believed that employees enjoy their mental and physical work duties.

    a. Design leadership
    b. Business Workflow Analysis
    c. Contingency theory
    d. Theory Y

23. Maslow's _____ is a theory in psychology, proposed by Abraham Maslow in his 1943 paper A Theory of Human Motivation, which he subsequently extended to include his observations of humans' innate curiosity.

Maslow's _____ is predetermined in order of importance. It is often depicted as a pyramid consisting of five levels: the lowest level is associated with physiological needs, while the uppermost level is associated with self-actualization needs, particularly those related to identity and purpose. Deficiency needs must be met first. Once these are met, seeking to satisfy growth needs drives personal growth. The higher needs in this hierarchy only come into focus when the lower needs in the pyramid are met.

    a. 33 Strategies of War
    b. 28-hour day
    c. 1990 Clean Air Act
    d. Hierarchy of needs

24. _____, is the discipline of using scientific research-based principles, strategies, and other analytical methods, such as mathematical modeling to improve any organization's ability to enact rational, meaningful business management decisions.
    a. Management science
    b. Cross ownership
    c. Trustee
    d. Workflow

25. _____ in the USA, Canada, South Africa and Australia, and operational research in Europe, is an interdisciplinary branch of applied mathematics and formal science that uses methods such as mathematical modeling, statistics, and algorithms to arrive at optimal or near optimal solutions to complex problems. It is typically concerned with optimizing the maxima (profit, assembly line performance, crop yield, bandwidth, etc) or minima (loss, risk, etc.) of some objective function.
    a. AAAI
    b. A4e
    c. A Stake in the Outcome
    d. Operations research

Chapter 2. Management Thought: Past and Present

26. _____ of the learning curve effect and the closely related experience curve effect express the relationship between equations for experience and efficiency or between efficiency gains and investment in the effort. The experience of 'learning curves' was first observed by the 19th Century German psychologist Hermann Ebbinghaus according to the difficulty of memorizing varying numbers of verbal stimuli, and subsequent learning about the complex processes of learning are discussed in the

.

The rule used for representing the learning curve effect states that the more times a task has been performed, the less time will be required on each subsequent iteration.

a. Spatial Decision Support Systems
b. Point biserial correlation coefficient
c. Models
d. Distribution

27. _____ is an area of business concerned with the production of goods and services, and involves the responsibility of ensuring that business operations are efficient in terms of using as little resource as needed, and effective in terms of meeting customer requirements. It is concerned with managing the process that converts inputs (in the forms of materials, labour and energy) into outputs (in the form of goods and services.)

Operations traditionally refers to the production of goods and services separately, although the distinction between these two main types of operations is increasingly difficult to make as manufacturers tend to merge product and service offerings.

a. A4e
b. AAAI
c. A Stake in the Outcome
d. Operations management

28. _____ is the process of recruiting individuals to fill executive positions in organizations. _____ may be performed by an organization's board of directors, by executives in the organization, or by an outside _____ organization.

The _____ profession has two distinct fields, retained _____ and contingency search.

a. Internet recruiting
b. Employee referral
c. Employment agency
d. Executive Search

29. _____ is an increasingly broadening term with which an organization, or other human system describes the combination of traditionally administrative personnel functions with acquisition and application of skills, knowledge and experience, Employee Relations and resource planning at various levels. The field draws upon concepts developed in Industrial/Organizational Psychology and System Theory. _____ has at least two related interpretations depending on context. The original usage derives from political economy and economics, where it was traditionally called labor, one of four factors of production although this perspective is changing as a function of new and ongoing research into more strategic approaches at national levels. This first usage is used more in terms of '_____ development', and can go beyond just organizations to the level of nations . The more traditional usage within corporations and businesses refers to the individuals within a firm or agency, and to the portion of the organization that deals with hiring, firing, training, and other personnel issues, typically referred to as `_____ management'.

Chapter 2. Management Thought: Past and Present

a. Progressive discipline	b. Human resource management
c. Bradford Factor	d. Human resources

30. _____ is a technical term used in management science popularized by Joseph M. Juran

He defined an internal and external customers as anyone affected by the product or by the process used to produce the product, in the context of quality management. _____s may play the role as supplier, processer, and customer in the sequence of product development.

He claimed that the organization must understand and identify both internal and external customers and their needs.

a. AAAI	b. Internal customer
c. A4e	d. A Stake in the Outcome

31. _____ is an integrated communications-based process through which individuals and communities discover that existing and newly-identified needs and wants may be satisfied by the products and services of others.

_____ is defined by the American _____ Association as the activity, set of institutions, and processes for creating, communicating, delivering, and exchanging offerings that have value for customers, clients, partners, and society at large. The term developed from the original meaning which referred literally to going to market, as in shopping, or going to a market to buy or sell goods or services.

a. Market development	b. Disruptive technology
c. Marketing	d. Customer relationship management

32. _____ is a strategic planning method used to evaluate the Strengths, Weaknesses, Opportunities, and Threats involved in a project or in a business venture. It involves specifying the objective of the business venture or project and identifying the internal and external factors that are favorable and unfavorable to achieving that objective. The technique is credited to Albert Humphrey, who led a convention at Stanford University in the 1960s and 1970s using data from Fortune 500 companies.

a. SWOT analysis	b. Marketing
c. Market share	d. Corporate image

33. _____ is the term used to describe a situation where different entities cooperate advantageously for a final outcome. Simply defined, it means that the whole is greater than the sum of the individual parts. Although the whole will be greater than each individual part, this is not the concept of _____.

a. 1990 Clean Air Act	b. Synergy
c. 28-hour day	d. 33 Strategies of War

34. In economics, business, retail, and accounting, a _____ is the value of money that has been used up to produce something, and hence is not available for use anymore. In economics, a _____ is an alternative that is given up as a result of a decision. In business, the _____ may be one of acquisition, in which case the amount of money expended to acquire it is counted as _____.

Chapter 2. Management Thought: Past and Present

a. Cost allocation
b. Fixed costs
c. Cost
d. Cost overrun

35. _____ is a Japanese philosophy that focuses on continuous improvement throughout all aspects of life. When applied to the workplace, _____ activities continually improve all functions of a business, from manufacturing to management and from the CEO to the assembly line workers. By improving standardized activities and processes, _____ aims to eliminate waste .
   a. Kaizen
   b. Sensitivity analysis
   c. Cross-docking
   d. Psychological pricing

36. _____ is the state or fact of exclusive rights and control over property, which may be an object, land/real estate or intellectual property. An _____ right is also referred to as title. The concept of _____ has existed for thousands of years and in all cultures.
   a. A4e
   b. Emanation of the state
   c. Ownership
   d. A Stake in the Outcome

37. In economics, and cost accounting, _____ describes the total economic cost of production and is made up of variable costs, which vary according to the quantity of a good produced and include inputs such as labor and raw materials, plus fixed costs, which are independent of the quantity of a good produced and include inputs (capital) that cannot be varied in the short term, such as buildings and machinery. _____ in economics includes the total opportunity cost of each factor of production in addition to fixed and variable costs.

The rate at which _____ changes as the amount produced changes is called marginal cost.

   a. 1990 Clean Air Act
   b. Total Cost
   c. 33 Strategies of War
   d. 28-hour day

38. _____ is a financial estimate designed to help consumers and enterprise managers assess direct and indirect costs It is a form of full cost accounting.
   a. Total Cost of Ownership
   b. 28-hour day
   c. 1990 Clean Air Act
   d. 33 Strategies of War

39. A _____ or business method is a collection of related, structured activities or tasks that produce a specific service or product (serve a particular goal) for a particular customer or customers. It often can be visualized with a flowchart as a sequence of activities.

There are three types of _____es:

1. Management processes, the processes that govern the operation of a system. Typical management processes include 'Corporate Governance' and 'Strategic Management'.
2. Operational processes, processes that constitute the core business and create the primary value stream. Typical operational processes are Purchasing, Manufacturing, Marketing, and Sales.
3. Supporting processes, which support the core processes. Examples include Accounting, Recruitment, Technical support.

A _____ begins with a customer's need and ends with a customer's need fulfillment. Process oriented organizations break down the barriers of structural departments and try to avoid functional silos.

   a. 1990 Clean Air Act
   b. 28-hour day
   c. 33 Strategies of War
   d. Business process

40. In probability theory, a probability distribution is called _____ if its cumulative distribution function is _____. This is equivalent to saying that for random variables X with the distribution in question, Pr[X = a] = 0 for all real numbers a, i.e.: the probability that X attains the value a is zero, for any number a. If the distribution of X is _____ then X is called a _____ random variable.

   a. Connectionist expert systems
   b. Decision tree pruning
   c. Pay Band
   d. Continuous

41. _____ is a management process whereby delivery (customer valued) processes are constantly evaluated and improved in the light of their efficiency, effectiveness and flexibility.

Some see it as a meta process for most management systems (Business Process Management, Quality Management, Project Management). Deming saw it as part of the 'system' whereby feedback from the process and customer were evaluated against organisational goals.

   a. Sole proprietorship
   b. Continuous Improvement Process
   c. Critical Success Factor
   d. First-mover advantage

42. In engineering and manufacturing, _____ and quality engineering are used in developing systems to ensure products or services are designed and produced to meet or exceed customer requirements. Refer to the definition by Merriam-Webster for further information. These systems are often developed in conjunction with other business and engineering disciplines using a cross-functional approach.

   a. Statistical process control
   b. Single Minute Exchange of Die
   c. Process capability
   d. Quality control

43. The _____ is the difference between the monetary value of exports and imports of output in an economy over a certain period of time. It is the relationship between a nation's imports and exports. A favourable _____ is known as a trade surplus and consists of exporting more than is imported; an unfavourable _____ is known as a trade deficit or, informally, a trade gap.

   a. Balance of trade
   b. Deregulation
   c. Value added
   d. Minimum wage

44. _____ is a company-wide computer software system used to manage and coordinate all the resources, information, and functions of a business from shared data stores.

An _____ system has a service-oriented architecture with modular hardware and software units and 'services' that communicate on a local area network. The modular design allows a business to add or reconfigure modules (perhaps from different vendors) while preserving data integrity in one shared database that may be centralized or distributed.

Chapter 2. Management Thought: Past and Present

a. Enterprise resource planning
b. A4e
c. A Stake in the Outcome
d. AAAI

45. _____ is an inventory strategy that strives to improve the return on investment of a business by reducing in-process inventory and its associated carrying costs. To meet _____ objectives, the process relies on signals between different points in the process. This means the process is often driven by a series of signals, or Kanban , which tell production when to make the next part. Kanban are usually 'tickets' but can be simple visual signals, such as the presence or absence of a part on a shelf. Implemented correctly, _____ can dramatically improve a manufacturing organization's return on investment, quality, and efficiency.

a. 28-hour day
b. 33 Strategies of War
c. Just-in-time
d. 1990 Clean Air Act

46. _____ or lean production, which is often known simply as 'Lean', is a production practice that considers the expenditure of resources for any goal other than the creation of value for the end customer to be wasteful, and thus a target for elimination. Working from the perspective of the customer who consumes a product or service, 'value' is defined as any action or process that a customer would be willing to pay for. Basically, lean is centered around creating more value with less work.

a. Six Sigma
b. Theory of constraints
c. Production line
d. Lean manufacturing

47. The _____ Automobile Company is an automobile manufacturer based in Wolfsburg, Germany, and is the original brand within the _____ Group, as well as the largest brand by sales volume.

_____ means 'people's car' in German, in which it is pronounced . Its current tagline or slogan is Das Auto .

a. Volkswagen
b. Competence-based Strategic Management
c. Turnover
d. Rate of return

48. _____ consists of the processes a company uses to track and organize its contacts with its current and prospective customers. _____ software is used to support these processes; information about customers and customer interactions can be entered, stored and accessed by employees in different company departments. Typical _____ goals are to improve services provided to customers, and to use customer contact information for targeted marketing.

a. Green marketing
b. Marketing plan
c. Customer relationship management
d. Disruptive technology

49. _____ describes commerce transactions between businesses, such as between a manufacturer and a wholesaler, or between a wholesaler and a retailer. Contrasting terms are business-to-consumer (B2C) and business-to-government (B2G.)

The volume of B2B transactions is much higher than the volume of B2C transactions.

a. Product bundling
b. Market environment
c. Category management
d. Business-to-business

50. Business-to-consumer describes activities of businesses serving end consumers with products and/or services.

An example of a _____ transaction would be a person buying a pair of shoes from a retailer. The transactions that led to the shoes being available for purchase, that is the purchase of the leather, laces, rubber, etc.

a. B2C
b. Green marketing
c. PEST analysis
d. Market environment

51. The _____ is the Cabinet department of the United States government concerned with promoting economic growth. It was originally created as the _____ and Labor on February 14, 1903. It was subsequently renamed to the Department of Commerce on March 4, 1913, and its bureaus and agencies specializing in labor were transferred to the new Department of Labor.

a. United States Department of Commerce
b. AAAI
c. A Stake in the Outcome
d. A4e

52. _____, commonly known as e-commerce, consists of the buying and selling of products or services over electronic systems such as the Internet and other computer networks. The amount of trade conducted electronically has grown extraordinarily with widespread Internet usage. The use of commerce is conducted in this way, spurring and drawing on innovations in electronic funds transfer, supply chain management, Internet marketing, online transaction processing, electronic data interchange (EDI), inventory management systems, and automated data collection systems.

a. Online shopping
b. A4e
c. A Stake in the Outcome
d. Electronic Commerce

53. _____ consists of the sale of goods or merchandise from a fixed location, such as a department store, boutique or kiosk in small or individual lots for direct consumption by the purchaser. _____ may include subordinated services, such as delivery. Purchasers may be individuals or businesses.

a. 28-hour day
b. 1990 Clean Air Act
c. Planogram
d. Retailing

54. _____ is an American writer on business management practices, best-known for, In Search of Excellence (co-authored with Robert H. Waterman, Jr.)

Peters was born in Baltimore, Maryland. He went to Severn School for High School and attended Cornell University, receiving a bachelor's degree in civil engineering in 1965, and a master's degree in 1966.

a. Affiliation
b. Adam Smith
c. Abraham Harold Maslow
d. Thomas J. Peters

55. _____ is exchange of capital, goods, and services across international borders or territories. In most countries, it represents a significant share of gross domestic product (GDP.) While _____ has been present throughout much of history, its economic, social, and political importance has been on the rise in recent centuries.

a. A4e
b. AAAI
c. International Trade
d. A Stake in the Outcome

Chapter 3. Management Ethics and Social Responsibility

1. _____ is a form of applied ethics that examines ethical principles and moral or ethical problems that arise in a business environment. It applies to all aspects of business conduct and is relevant to the conduct of individuals and business organizations as a whole. Applied ethics is a field of ethics that deals with ethical questions in many fields such as medical, technical, legal and _____.
   - a. Hypernorms
   - b. Corporate Sustainability
   - c. Facilitation payments
   - d. Business ethics

2. _____, commonly known as e-commerce, consists of the buying and selling of products or services over electronic systems such as the Internet and other computer networks. The amount of trade conducted electronically has grown extraordinarily with widespread Internet usage. The use of commerce is conducted in this way, spurring and drawing on innovations in electronic funds transfer, supply chain management, Internet marketing, online transaction processing, electronic data interchange (EDI), inventory management systems, and automated data collection systems.
   - a. A Stake in the Outcome
   - b. Online shopping
   - c. A4e
   - d. Electronic commerce

3. The _____ of 2002 (Pub.L. 107-204, 116 Stat. 745, enacted July 30, 2002), also known as the Public Company Accounting Reform and Investor Protection Act of 2002 and commonly called Sarbanes-Oxley, Sarbox or SOX, is a United States federal law enacted on July 30, 2002, as a reaction to a number of major corporate and accounting scandals including those affecting Enron, Tyco International, Adelphia, Peregrine Systems and WorldCom.
   - a. Fair Labor Standards Act
   - b. Sarbanes-Oxley Act
   - c. Sarbanes-Oxley Act of 2002
   - d. Letter of credit

4. The _____, also known as the Public Company Accounting Reform and Investor Protection Act of 2002 and commonly called Sarbanes-Oxley, Sarbox or SOX, is a United States federal law enacted on July 30, 2002, as a reaction to a number of major corporate and accounting scandals including those affecting Enron, Tyco International, Adelphia, Peregrine Systems and WorldCom.
   - a. Munn v. Illinois
   - b. Letter of credit
   - c. MacPherson v. Buick Motor Co.
   - d. Sarbanes-Oxley Act of 2002

5. The U.S. _____ is an independent agency of the United States government which holds primary responsibility for enforcing the federal securities laws and regulating the securities industry, the nation's stock and options exchanges, and other electronic securities markets. The SEC was created by section 4 of the Securities Exchange Act of 1934 (now codified as 15 U.S.C. Â§ 78d and commonly referred to as the 1934 Act.)
   - a. 33 Strategies of War
   - b. 1990 Clean Air Act
   - c. Securities and Exchange Commission
   - d. 28-hour day

6. _____ is one of the managerial functions like planning, organizing, staffing and directing. It is an important function because it helps to check the errors and to take the corrective action so that deviation from standards are minimized and stated goals of the organization are achieved in desired manner. According to modern concepts, _____ is a foreseeing action whereas earlier concept of _____ was used only when errors were detected. _____ in management means setting standards, measuring actual performance and taking corrective action.
   - a. Schedule of reinforcement
   - b. Decision tree pruning
   - c. Turnover
   - d. Control

7. The _____ is a politically conservative group of chief executive officers of major U.S. corporations formed to promote pro-business public policy.

Chapter 3. Management Ethics and Social Responsibility

The group was formed in 1972 through the merger of three existing organizations: the March Group, consisting of chief executive officers who met informally to consider public policy issues; the Construction Users Anti-Inflation Roundtable, a group devoted to containing construction costs; and the Labor Law Study Committee, largely made up of labor relations executives of major companies.

It 'strongly supported passage of the' No Child Left Behind Act of 2002, 'and is now actively working with states on implementation.' It has issued press releases, submitted editorials, given congressional testimony and distributed position ads.

a. Process-based management
b. Business Roundtable
c. National Association for the Advancement of Colored People
d. Headquarters

8. The _____, widely known as ISO , is an international-standard-setting body composed of representatives from various national standards organizations. Founded on 23 February 1947, the organization promulgates worldwide proprietary industrial and commercial standards. It is headquartered in Geneva, Switzerland.

a. A4e
b. International Organization for Standardization
c. AAAI
d. A Stake in the Outcome

9. _____ is a contract between two parties, one being the employer and the other being the employee. An employee may be defined as: 'A person in the service of another under any contract of hire, express or implied, oral or written, where the employer has the power or right to control and direct the employee in the material details of how the work is to be performed.' Black's Law Dictionary page 471 (5th ed. 1979.)

a. Exit interview
b. Employment counsellor
c. Employment rate
d. Employment

10. The term _____ was created by President Lyndon B. Johnson when he signed Executive Order 11246 on September 24, 1965, created to prohibit federal contractors from discriminating against employees on the basis of race, sex, creed, religion, color, or national origin. In more recent times, most employers have also added sexual orientation to the list of non-discrimination.

The Executive Order also required contractors to implement affirmative action plans to increase the participation of minorities and women in the workplace.

a. A4e
b. A Stake in the Outcome
c. Equal Employment Opportunity
d. AAAI

11. The U.S. _____ is a federal agency whose goal is ending employment discrimination. The _____ investigates discrimination complaints based on an individual's race, color, national origin, religion, sex, age, disability and retaliation for reporting and/or opposing a discriminatory practice. The Commission is also tasked with filing suits on behalf of alleged victim(s) of discrimination against employers and as an adjudicatory for claims of discrimination brought against federal agencies.

a. Airbus Industrie
b. Equal Employment Opportunity Commission
c. ARCO
d. Airbus SAS

Chapter 3. Management Ethics and Social Responsibility

12. An _____ is a situation that will often involve an apparent conflict between moral imperatives, in which to obey one would result in transgressing another. This is also called an ethical paradox since in moral philosophy, paradox plays a central role in ethics debates. For instance, an ethical admonition to 'love thy neighbour as thy self' is not always just in contrast with, but sometimes in contradiction to an armed neighbour actively trying to kill you: if he or she succeeds, you will not be able to love him or her.

   a. Ethical dilemma
   b. A Stake in the Outcome
   c. A4e
   d. AAAI

13. _____ is an integrated communications-based process through which individuals and communities discover that existing and newly-identified needs and wants may be satisfied by the products and services of others.

   _____ is defined by the American _____ Association as the activity, set of institutions, and processes for creating, communicating, delivering, and exchanging offerings that have value for customers, clients, partners, and society at large. The term developed from the original meaning which referred literally to going to market, as in shopping, or going to a market to buy or sell goods or services.

   a. Market development
   b. Customer relationship management
   c. Disruptive technology
   d. Marketing

14. _____ is a form of marketing developed from direct response marketing campaigns conducted in the 1970s and 1980s which emphasizes customer retention and satisfaction, rather than a dominant focus on point-of-sale transactions.

   _____ differs from other forms of marketing in that it recognizes the long term value to the firm of keeping customers, as opposed to direct or 'Intrusion' marketing, which focuses upon acquisition of new clients by targeting majority demographics based upon prospective client lists.

   _____ refers to a long-term and mutually beneficial arrangement wherein both the buyer and seller focus on value enhancement with the goal of providing a more satisfying exchange.

   a. 1990 Clean Air Act
   b. 28-hour day
   c. Relationship Marketing
   d. Guerrilla marketing

15. The _____ was a period in the late 18th and early 19th centuries when major changes in agriculture, manufacturing, mining, and transportation had a profound effect on the socioeconomic and cultural conditions in Britain. The changes subsequently spread throughout Europe, North America, and eventually the world. The onset of the _____ marked a major turning point in human society; almost every aspect of daily life was eventually influenced in some way.

   a. Adam Smith
   b. Industrial Revolution
   c. Abraham Harold Maslow
   d. Affiliation

16. _____ is the process of recruiting individuals to fill executive positions in organizations. _____ may be performed by an organization's board of directors, by executives in the organization, or by an outside _____ organization.

   The _____ profession has two distinct fields, retained _____ and contingency search.

a. Internet recruiting
b. Employment agency
c. Executive Search
d. Employee referral

17. The _____, 5 U.S.C. § 552a, establishes a code of fair information practices that governs the collection, maintenance, use, and dissemination of personally identifiable information about individuals that is maintained in systems of records by federal agencies. A system of records is a group of records under the control of an agency from which information is retrieved by the name of the individual or by some identifier assigned to the individual.
   a. Negligence
   b. Privacy Act of 1974
   c. Personal Responsibility and Work Opportunity Reconciliation Act
   d. No-FEAR Act

18. The 'business case for _____', theorizes that in a global marketplace, a company that employs a diverse workforce (both men and women, people of many generations, people from ethnically and racially diverse backgrounds etc.) is better able to understand the demographics of the marketplace it serves and is thus better equipped to thrive in that marketplace than a company that has a more limited range of employee demographics.

An additional corollary suggests that a company that supports the _____ of its workforce can also improve employee satisfaction, productivity and retention.

   a. Kanban
   b. Trademark
   c. Virtual team
   d. Diversity

19. An _____ is a private network that uses Internet protocols, network connectivity, and possibly the public telecommunication system to securely share part of an organization's information or operations with suppliers, vendors, partners, customers or other businesses. An _____ can be viewed as part of a company's intranet that is extended to users outside the company (e.g.: normally over the Internet.) It has also been described as a 'state of mind' in which the Internet is perceived as a way to do business with a preapproved set of other companies business-to-business (B2B), in isolation from all other Internet users.
   a. A Stake in the Outcome
   b. A4e
   c. Extranet
   d. AAAI

20. An _____ is a private computer network that uses Internet technologies to securely share any part of an organization's information or operational systems with its employees. Sometimes the term refers only to the organization's internal website, but often it is a more extensive part of the organization's computer infrastructure and private websites are an important component and focal point of internal communication and collaboration.

An _____ is built from the same concepts and technologies used for the Internet, such as client-server computing and the Internet Protocol Suite (TCP/IP.)

   a. A4e
   b. Intranet
   c. A Stake in the Outcome
   d. AAAI

21. In game theory, an _____ is a set of moves or strategies taken by the players, or their payoffs resulting from the actions or strategies taken by all players. The two are complementary in that given knowledge of the set of strategies of all players, the final state of the game is known, as are any relevant payoffs. In a game where chance or a random event is involved, the _____ is not known from only the set of strategies, but is only realized when the random event(s) are realized.
- a. A Stake in the Outcome
- b. A4e
- c. Outcome
- d. AAAI

22. The _____ is a piece of United States environmental policy relating to the reduction of smog and air pollution. It follows the Clean Air Act in 1963, the Clean Air Act Amendment in 1966, the Clean Air Act Extension in 1970, and the Clean Air Act Amendments in 1977. It was enacted by the 101st United States Congress (Pub.L.
- a. Family and Medical Leave Act of 1993
- b. Robinson-Patman Act
- c. Reverification
- d. 1990 Clean Air Act

23. The _____ is an agency of the United States Department of Health and Human Services and is responsible for regulating and supervising the safety of foods, dietary supplements, drugs, vaccines, biological medical products, blood products, medical devices, radiation-emitting devices, veterinary products, and cosmetics. The FDA also enforces section 361 of the Public Health Service Act and the associated regulations, including sanitation requirements on interstate travel as well as specific rules for control of disease on products ranging from pet turtles to semen donations for assisted reproductive medicine techniques.

The FDA is an agency within the United States Department of Health and Human Services responsible for protecting and promoting the nation's public health.

- a. 28-hour day
- b. 1990 Clean Air Act
- c. 33 Strategies of War
- d. Food and Drug Administration

24. _____ can be considered to have three main components: quality control, quality assurance and quality improvement. _____ is focused not only on product quality, but also the means to achieve it. _____ therefore uses quality assurance and control of processes as well as products to achieve more consistent quality.
- a. Total quality management
- b. 1990 Clean Air Act
- c. Quality Management
- d. 28-hour day

25. The general definition of an _____ is an evaluation of a person, organization, system, process, project or product. _____s are performed to ascertain the validity and reliability of information; also to provide an assessment of a system's internal control. The goal of an _____ is to express an opinion on the person / organization/system (etc) in question, under evaluation based on work done on a test basis.
- a. Audit
- b. Audit committee
- c. A Stake in the Outcome
- d. Internal control

26. _____ is an advertisement in which a particular product specifically mentions a competitor by name for the express purpose of showing why the competitor is inferior to the product naming it.

This should not be confused with parody advertisements, where a fictional product is being advertised for the purpose of poking fun at the particular advertisement, nor should it be confused with the use of a coined brand name for the purpose of comparing the product without actually naming an actual competitor. ('Wikipedia tastes better and is less filling than the Encyclopedia Galactica.')

In the 1980s, during what has been referred to as the cola wars, soft-drink manufacturer Pepsi ran a series of advertisements where people, caught on hidden camera, in a blind taste test, chose Pepsi over rival Coca-Cola.

a. Comparative advertising
b. 28-hour day
c. 1990 Clean Air Act
d. 33 Strategies of War

Chapter 4. Management`s Commitment to Quality and Productivity 25

1. _____ is the process of recruiting individuals to fill executive positions in organizations. _____ may be performed by an organization's board of directors, by executives in the organization, or by an outside _____ organization.

The _____ profession has two distinct fields, retained _____ and contingency search.

   a. Employment agency   b. Internet recruiting
   c. Employee referral   d. Executive Search

2. _____, a business term, is a measure of how products and services supplied by a company meet or surpass customer expectation. It is seen as a key performance indicator within business and is part of the four perspectives of a Balanced Scorecard.

In a competitive marketplace where businesses compete for customers, _____ is seen as a key differentiator and increasingly has become a key element of business strategy.

   a. Horizontal integration   b. Foreign ownership
   c. Customer Satisfaction   d. Critical Success Factor

3. In economics, business, retail, and accounting, a _____ is the value of money that has been used up to produce something, and hence is not available for use anymore. In economics, a _____ is an alternative that is given up as a result of a decision. In business, the _____ may be one of acquisition, in which case the amount of money expended to acquire it is counted as _____.

   a. Fixed costs   b. Cost allocation
   c. Cost overrun   d. Cost

4. _____ is the state or fact of exclusive rights and control over property, which may be an object, land/real estate or intellectual property. An _____ right is also referred to as title. The concept of _____ has existed for thousands of years and in all cultures.

   a. Emanation of the state   b. Ownership
   c. A4e   d. A Stake in the Outcome

5. In economics, and cost accounting, _____ describes the total economic cost of production and is made up of variable costs, which vary according to the quantity of a good produced and include inputs such as labor and raw materials, plus fixed costs, which are independent of the quantity of a good produced and include inputs (capital) that cannot be varied in the short term, such as buildings and machinery. _____ in economics includes the total opportunity cost of each factor of production in addition to fixed and variable costs.

The rate at which _____ changes as the amount produced changes is called marginal cost.

   a. 1990 Clean Air Act   b. Total Cost
   c. 33 Strategies of War   d. 28-hour day

6. _____ is a financial estimate designed to help consumers and enterprise managers assess direct and indirect costs It is a form of full cost accounting.

   a. Total Cost of Ownership   b. 1990 Clean Air Act
   c. 28-hour day   d. 33 Strategies of War

Chapter 4. Management's Commitment to Quality and Productivity

7. _____ is an advertisement in which a particular product specifically mentions a competitor by name for the express purpose of showing why the competitor is inferior to the product naming it.

This should not be confused with parody advertisements, where a fictional product is being advertised for the purpose of poking fun at the particular advertisement, nor should it be confused with the use of a coined brand name for the purpose of comparing the product without actually naming an actual competitor. ('Wikipedia tastes better and is less filling than the Encyclopedia Galactica.')

In the 1980s, during what has been referred to as the cola wars, soft-drink manufacturer Pepsi ran a series of advertisements where people, caught on hidden camera, in a blind taste test, chose Pepsi over rival Coca-Cola.

a. 33 Strategies of War
b. 28-hour day
c. 1990 Clean Air Act
d. Comparative advertising

8. _____ is one of the managerial functions like planning, organizing, staffing and directing. It is an important function because it helps to check the errors and to take the corrective action so that deviation from standards are minimized and stated goals of the organization are achieved in desired manner. According to modern concepts, _____ is a foreseeing action whereas earlier concept of _____ was used only when errors were detected. _____ in management means setting standards, measuring actual performance and taking corrective action.

a. Control
b. Schedule of reinforcement
c. Decision tree pruning
d. Turnover

9. In engineering and manufacturing, _____ and quality engineering are used in developing systems to ensure products or services are designed and produced to meet or exceed customer requirements. Refer to the definition by Merriam-Webster for further information . These systems are often developed in conjunction with other business and engineering disciplines using a cross-functional approach.

a. Process capability
b. Single Minute Exchange of Die
c. Statistical process control
d. Quality control

10. Procter is a surname, and may also refer to:

- Bryan Waller Procter (pseud. Barry Cornwall), English poet
- Goodwin Procter, American law firm
- _____, consumer products multinational

a. Master and Servant Acts
b. Downstream
c. Procter ' Gamble
d. Strict liability

11. _____ is a Fortune 500, American multinational corporation headquartered in Cincinnati, Ohio, that manufactures a wide range of consumer goods. As of 2008, P'G is the 8th largest corporation in the world by market capitalization and 14th largest US company by profit.

a. Procter ' Gamble Co.
b. Turnover
c. Maturity of Organizations and Business Excellence - The Four-Phase Model
d. STAR

Chapter 4. Management's Commitment to Quality and Productivity

12. _____ refers to metrics and measures of output from production processes, per unit of input. Labor _____, for example, is typically measured as a ratio of output per labor-hour, an input. _____ may be conceived of as a metrics of the technical or engineering efficiency of production.
    a. Master production schedule
    b. Remanufacturing
    c. Productivity
    d. Value engineering

13. _____ is a Japanese philosophy that focuses on continuous improvement throughout all aspects of life. When applied to the workplace, _____ activities continually improve all functions of a business, from manufacturing to management and from the CEO to the assembly line workers. By improving standardized activities and processes, _____ aims to eliminate waste .
    a. Cross-docking
    b. Sensitivity analysis
    c. Kaizen
    d. Psychological pricing

14. _____ is a form of applied ethics that examines ethical principles and moral or ethical problems that arise in a business environment. It applies to all aspects of business conduct and is relevant to the conduct of individuals and business organizations as a whole. Applied ethics is a field of ethics that deals with ethical questions in many fields such as medical, technical, legal and _____.
    a. Hypernorms
    b. Corporate Sustainability
    c. Facilitation payments
    d. Business Ethics

15. _____ is a structured approach to transitioning individuals, teams, and organizations from a current state to a desired future state. The current definition of _____ includes both organizational _____ processes and individual _____ models, which together are used to manage the people side of change.

    A number of models are available for understanding the transitioning of individuals through the phases of _____ and strengthening organizational development initiative in both government and corporate sectors.

    a. 28-hour day
    b. 33 Strategies of War
    c. 1990 Clean Air Act
    d. Change management

16. _____ is a set of values based on hard work and diligence. It is also a belief in the moral benefit of work and its ability to enhance character. An example would be the Protestant _____.
    a. 1990 Clean Air Act
    b. 33 Strategies of War
    c. Work ethic
    d. 28-hour day

17. _____ has been described as the 'process of social influence in which one person can enlist the aid and support of others in the accomplishment of a common task' . A definition more inclusive of followers comes from Alan Keith of Genentech who said '_____ is ultimately about creating a way for people to contribute to making something extraordinary happen.'

    _____ is one of the most salient aspects of the organizational context. However, defining _____ has been challenging.

    a. 28-hour day
    b. 1990 Clean Air Act
    c. Situational leadership
    d. Leadership

Chapter 4. Management's Commitment to Quality and Productivity

18. A _____ is a brief written statement of the purpose of a company or organization. Ideally, a _____ guides the actions of the organization, spells out its overall goal, provides a sense of direction, and guides decision making for all levels of management.

_____s often contain the following:

- Purpose and aim of the organization
- The organization's primary stakeholders: clients, stockholders, etc.
- Responsibilities of the organization toward these stakeholders
- Products and services offered

In developing a _____:

- Encourage as much input as feasible from employees, volunteers, and other stakeholders
- Publicize it broadly

The _____ can be used to resolve differences between business stakeholders. Stakeholders include: employees including managers and executives, stockholders, board of directors, customers, suppliers, distributors, creditors, governments (local, state, federal, etc.), unions, competitors, NGO's, and the general public.

a. 28-hour day
b. Mission statement
c. 1990 Clean Air Act
d. 33 Strategies of War

19. _____ is a management technique pioneered by Michael Phillips in San Francisco in the late '60's and early '70s. The concept's most visible success was by Jack Stack and his team at SRC Holdings and popularized in 1995 by John Case. The technique is to give employees all relevant financial information about the company so they can make better decisions as workers.

a. Open-book management
b. AAAI
c. A4e
d. A Stake in the Outcome

20. In game theory, an _____ is a set of moves or strategies taken by the players, or their payoffs resulting from the actions or strategies taken by all players. The two are complementary in that given knowledge of the set of strategies of all players, the final state of the game is known, as are any relevant payoffs. In a game where chance or a random event is involved, the _____ is not known from only the set of strategies, but is only realized when the random event(s) are realized.

a. AAAI
b. Outcome
c. A Stake in the Outcome
d. A4e

21. _____ is the process of disassembly and recovery at the module level and, eventually, at the component level. It requires the repair or replacement of worn out or obsolete components and modules. Parts subject to degradation affecting the performance or the expected life of the whole are replaced.

a. Productivity
b. Capacity planning
c. Methods-time measurement
d. ReManufacturing

Chapter 4. Management's Commitment to Quality and Productivity

22. _____ is a strategic planning method used to evaluate the Strengths, Weaknesses, Opportunities, and Threats involved in a project or in a business venture. It involves specifying the objective of the business venture or project and identifying the internal and external factors that are favorable and unfavorable to achieving that objective. The technique is credited to Albert Humphrey, who led a convention at Stanford University in the 1960s and 1970s using data from Fortune 500 companies.

   a. Corporate image
   b. SWOT analysis
   c. Marketing
   d. Market share

23. _____, widely known as F. W. Taylor, was an American mechanical engineer who sought to improve industrial efficiency. He is regarded as the father of scientific management, and was one of the first management consultants.

Taylor was one of the intellectual leaders of the Efficiency Movement and his ideas, broadly conceived, were highly influential in the Progressive Era.

   a. Geoffrey Colvin
   b. Frederick Winslow Taylor
   c. Douglas N. Daft
   d. Jonah Jacob Goldberg

24. _____ refers to increasing the spiritual, political, social or economic strength of individuals and communities. It often involves the empowered developing confidence in their own capacities.

The term Human _____ covers a vast landscape of meanings, interpretations, definitions and disciplines ranging from psychology and philosophy to the highly commercialized Self-Help industry and Motivational sciences.

   a. A4e
   b. AAAI
   c. Empowerment
   d. A Stake in the Outcome

25. _____ is a layer of management in an organization whose primary job responsibility is to monitor activities of subordinates while reporting to upper management.

In pre-computer times, _____ would collect information from junior management and reassemble it for senior management. With the advent of inexpensive PCs this function has been taken over by e-business systems.

   a. Continuous monitoring
   b. Theory Y
   c. Community management
   d. Middle management

26. _____ is subcontracting a process, such as product design or manufacturing, to a third-party company. The decision to outsource is often made in the interest of lowering cost or making better use of time and energy costs, redirecting or conserving energy directed at the competencies of a particular business, or to make more efficient use of land, labor, capital, (information) technology and resources. _____ became part of the business lexicon during the 1980s.

   a. Outsourcing
   b. Opinion leadership
   c. Operant conditioning
   d. Unemployment insurance

27. _____ is the term used to describe a situation where different entities cooperate advantageously for a final outcome. Simply defined, it means that the whole is greater than the sum of the individual parts. Although the whole will be greater than each individual part, this is not the concept of _____.

Chapter 4. Management's Commitment to Quality and Productivity

a. 1990 Clean Air Act
b. 28-hour day
c. 33 Strategies of War
d. Synergy

28. In organizational development (OD), _____ is a series of actions taken by a Process Owner to identify, analyze and improve existing processes within an organization to meet new goals and objectives. These actions often follow a specific methodology or strategy to create successful results. A sampling of these are listed below.
a. Letter of resignation
b. Product innovation
c. Supervisory board
d. Process improvement

29. Quality management can be considered to have three main components: quality control, quality assurance and _____. Quality management is focused not only on product quality, but also the means to achieve it. Quality management therefore uses quality assurance and control of processes as well as products to achieve more consistent quality.
a. 1990 Clean Air Act
b. 28-hour day
c. Quality management
d. Quality improvement

30. The _____ is given by the United States National Institute of Standards and Technology. Through the actions of the National Productivity Advisory Committee chaired by Jack Grayson, it was established by the Malcolm Baldrige National Quality Improvement Act of 1987 - Public Law 100-107 and named for Malcolm Baldrige, who served as United States Secretary of Commerce during the Reagan administration from 1981 until his 1987 death in a rodeo accident. APQC, , organized the first White House Conference on Productivity, spearheading the creation and design of the _____ in 1987, and jointly administering the award for its first three years.
a. Business Network Transformation
b. Scenario planning
c. Time and attendance
d. Malcolm Baldrige National Quality Award

31. The general definition of an _____ is an evaluation of a person, organization, system, process, project or product. _____s are performed to ascertain the validity and reliability of information; also to provide an assessment of a system's internal control. The goal of an _____ is to express an opinion on the person / organization/system (etc) in question, under evaluation based on work done on a test basis.
a. Audit
b. A Stake in the Outcome
c. Audit committee
d. Internal control

32. A _____ is a group of employees from various functional areas of the organization - research, engineering, marketing, finance. human resources, and operations, for example - who are all focused on a specific objective and are responsible to work as a team to improve coordination and innovation across divisions and resolve mutual problems.
a. Goal-setting theory
b. Graduate recruitment
c. Sociotechnical systems
d. Cross-functional team

Chapter 4. Management's Commitment to Quality and Productivity

33. _____ refers to the movement of cash into or out of a business or financial product. It is usually measured during a specified, finite period of time. Measurement of _____ can be used

- to determine a project's rate of return or value. The time of _____s into and out of projects are used as inputs in financial models such as internal rate of return, and net present value.
- to determine problems with a business's liquidity. Being profitable does not necessarily mean being liquid. A company can fail because of a shortage of cash, even while profitable.
- as an alternate measure of a business's profits when it is believed that accrual accounting concepts do not represent economic realities. For example, a company may be notionally profitable but generating little operational cash (as may be the case for a company that barters its products rather than selling for cash.) In such a case, the company may be deriving additional operating cash by issuing shares evaluating default risk, re-investment requirements, etc.

_____ is a generic term used differently depending on the context. It may be defined by users for their own purposes.

a. Gross profit margin
b. Sweat equity
c. Cash flow
d. Gross profit

34. A _____ is a volunteer group composed of workers (or even students), usually under the leadership of their supervisor (but they can elect a team leader), who are trained to identify, analyse and solve work-related problems and present their solutions to management in order to improve the performance of the organization, and motivate and enrich the work of employees. When matured, true _____s become self-managing, having gained the confidence of management.
_____s are an alternative to the dehumanising concept of the Division of Labour, where workers or individuals are treated like robots.

a. Quality circle
b. Connectionist expert systems
c. Competency-based job descriptions
d. Certified in Production and Inventory Management

35. _____ is an effective method of monitoring a process through the use of control charts. Control charts enable the use of objective criteria for distinguishing background variation from events of significance based on statistical techniques. Much of its power lies in the ability to monitor both process center and its variation about that center.

a. Statistical process control
b. Process capability
c. Single Minute Exchange of Die
d. Quality control

36. _____ is an integrated communications-based process through which individuals and communities discover that existing and newly-identified needs and wants may be satisfied by the products and services of others.

_____ is defined by the American _____ Association as the activity, set of institutions, and processes for creating, communicating, delivering, and exchanging offerings that have value for customers, clients, partners, and society at large. The term developed from the original meaning which referred literally to going to market, as in shopping, or going to a market to buy or sell goods or services.

a. Customer relationship management
b. Disruptive technology
c. Market development
d. Marketing

Chapter 4. Management's Commitment to Quality and Productivity

37. A _____ is a type of business entity in which partners (owners) share with each other the profits or losses of the business. _____s are often favored over corporations for taxation purposes, as the _____ structure does not generally incur a tax on profits before it is distributed to the partners (i.e. there is no dividend tax levied.) However, depending on the _____ structure and the jurisdiction in which it operates, owners of a _____ may be exposed to greater personal liability than they would as shareholders of a corporation.
   - a. Mediation
   - b. Federal Employers Liability Act
   - c. Due process
   - d. Partnership

38. _____ is a form of marketing developed from direct response marketing campaigns conducted in the 1970s and 1980s which emphasizes customer retention and satisfaction, rather than a dominant focus on point-of-sale transactions.

   _____ differs from other forms of marketing in that it recognizes the long term value to the firm of keeping customers, as opposed to direct or 'Intrusion' marketing, which focuses upon acquisition of new clients by targeting majority demographics based upon prospective client lists.

   _____ refers to a long-term and mutually beneficial arrangement wherein both the buyer and seller focus on value enhancement with the goal of providing a more satisfying exchange.

   - a. Relationship Marketing
   - b. 1990 Clean Air Act
   - c. Guerrilla marketing
   - d. 28-hour day

39. The phrase _____, according to the Organization for Economic Co-operation and Development, refers to 'creative work undertaken on a systematic basis in order to increase the stock of knowledge, including knowledge of man, culture and society, and the use of this stock of knowledge to devise new applications [sic]'

   New product design and development is more than often a crucial factor in the survival of a company. In an industry that is fast changing, firms must continually revise their design and range of products. This is necessary due to continuous technology change and development as well as other competitors and the changing preference of customers.

   - a. 28-hour day
   - b. Research and development
   - c. 1990 Clean Air Act
   - d. 33 Strategies of War

40. _____ is the process of comparing the cost, cycle time, productivity, or quality of a specific process or method to another that is widely considered to be an industry standard or best practice. Essentially, _____ provides a snapshot of the performance of your business and helps you understand where you are in relation to a particular standard. The result is often a business case for making changes in order to make improvements.
   - a. Cost leadership
   - b. Benchmarking
   - c. Competitive heterogeneity
   - d. Complementors

41. In probability theory, a probability distribution is called _____ if its cumulative distribution function is _____. This is equivalent to saying that for random variables X with the distribution in question, Pr[X = a] = 0 for all real numbers a, i.e.: the probability that X attains the value a is zero, for any number a. If the distribution of X is _____ then X is called a _____ random variable.

a. Decision tree pruning
b. Continuous
c. Connectionist expert systems
d. Pay Band

42. _____ is a management process whereby delivery (customer valued) processes are constantly evaluated and improved in the light of their efficiency, effectiveness and flexibility.

Some see it as a meta process for most management systems (Business Process Management, Quality Management, Project Management). Deming saw it as part of the 'system' whereby feedback from the process and customer were evaluated against organisational goals.

a. Sole proprietorship
b. Critical Success Factor
c. First-mover advantage
d. Continuous Improvement Process

43. _____ is an inventory strategy that strives to improve the return on investment of a business by reducing in-process inventory and its associated carrying costs. To meet _____ objectives, the process relies on signals between different points in the process. This means the process is often driven by a series of signals, or Kanban, which tell production when to make the next part. Kanban are usually 'tickets' but can be simple visual signals, such as the presence or absence of a part on a shelf. Implemented correctly, _____ can dramatically improve a manufacturing organization's return on investment, quality, and efficiency.

a. 1990 Clean Air Act
b. Just-in-time
c. 33 Strategies of War
d. 28-hour day

Chapter 5. The Manager's Environment

1. _____ is the largest book retailer in the United States, operating mainly through its Barnes ' Noble Booksellers chain of bookstores headquartered in lower Fifth Avenue in Manhattan.

The company operates the chain of small 'B.

   a. 1990 Clean Air Act
   c. 33 Strategies of War
   b. 28-hour day
   d. Barnes ' Noble, Inc.

2. _____, a business term, is a measure of how products and services supplied by a company meet or surpass customer expectation. It is seen as a key performance indicator within business and is part of the four perspectives of a Balanced Scorecard.

In a competitive marketplace where businesses compete for customers, _____ is seen as a key differentiator and increasingly has become a key element of business strategy.

   a. Horizontal integration
   c. Customer Satisfaction
   b. Foreign ownership
   d. Critical Success Factor

3. _____, commonly known as e-commerce, consists of the buying and selling of products or services over electronic systems such as the Internet and other computer networks. The amount of trade conducted electronically has grown extraordinarily with widespread Internet usage. The use of commerce is conducted in this way, spurring and drawing on innovations in electronic funds transfer, supply chain management, Internet marketing, online transaction processing, electronic data interchange (EDI), inventory management systems, and automated data collection systems.

   a. Electronic commerce
   c. A4e
   b. Online shopping
   d. A Stake in the Outcome

4. _____ is a process of gathering, analyzing, and dispensing information for tactical or strategic purposes. The _____ process entails obtaining both factual and subjective information on the business environments in which a company is operating or considering entering.

There are three ways of scanning the business environment:

- Ad-hoc scanning - Short term, infrequent examinations usually initiated by a crisis
- Regular scanning - Studies done on a regular schedule (say, once a year)
- Continuous scanning(also called continuous learning) - continuous structured data collection and processing on a broad range of environmental factors

Most commentators feel that in today's turbulent business environment the best scanning method available is continuous scanning. This allows the firm to :

-act quickly-take advantage of opportunities before competitors do-respond to environmental threats before significant damage is done

   a. A Stake in the Outcome
   c. AAAI
   b. A4e
   d. Environmental scanning

5. _____ is the process of recruiting individuals to fill executive positions in organizations. _____ may be performed by an organization's board of directors, by executives in the organization, or by an outside _____ organization.

The _____ profession has two distinct fields, retained _____ and contingency search.

   a. Employee referral
   b. Internet recruiting
   c. Executive Search
   d. Employment agency

6. _____ is something that a firm can do well and that meets the following three conditions:

Competencies are things that companys execute well across several business units or product sectors.

Firms usually have few competencies, but these are usually less liable to change rapidly.

1. It provides consumer benefits
2. It is not easy for competitors to imitate
3. It can be leveraged widely to many products and markets.

A _____ can take various forms, including technical/subject matter know-how, a reliable process and/or close relationships with customers and suppliers (Mascarenhas et al. 1998.)

   a. Learning-by-doing
   b. Dominant Design
   c. NAIRU
   d. Core competency

7. The 'business case for _____', theorizes that in a global marketplace, a company that employs a diverse workforce (both men and women, people of many generations, people from ethnically and racially diverse backgrounds etc.) is better able to understand the demographics of the marketplace it serves and is thus better equipped to thrive in that marketplace than a company that has a more limited range of employee demographics.

An additional corollary suggests that a company that supports the _____ of its workforce can also improve employee satisfaction, productivity and retention.

   a. Trademark
   b. Virtual team
   c. Kanban
   d. Diversity

8. The term _____ collectively refers to all resources that determine the value and the competitiveness of an enterprise. As such, it includes as subsets the attributes that concur to building all financial statements as well as the balance sheet.

   a. A Stake in the Outcome
   b. AAAI
   c. Intellectual capital
   d. A4e

9. _____ is an idea in the field of Organizational studies and management which describes the psychology, attitudes, experiences, beliefs and Values (personal and cultural values) of an organization. It has been defined as 'the specific collection of values and norms that are shared by people and groups in an organization and that control the way they interact with each other and with stakeholders outside the organization.'

Chapter 5. The Manager's Environment

This definition continues to explain organizational values also known as 'beliefs and ideas about what kinds of goals members of an organization should pursue and ideas about the appropriate kinds or standards of behavior organizational members should use to achieve these goals. From organizational values develop organizational norms, guidelines or expectations that prescribe appropriate kinds of behavior by employees in particular situations and control the behavior of organizational members towards one another.'

_____ is not the same as corporate culture.

a. Union shop
c. Organizational effectiveness
b. Organizational development
d. Organizational culture

10. In sociology, anthropology and cultural studies, a _____ is a group of people with a culture (whether distinct or hidden) which differentiates them from the larger culture to which they belong. If a particular _____ is characterized by a systematic opposition to the dominant culture, it may be described as a counterculture.

As early as 1950, David Riesman distinguished between a majority, 'which passively accepted commercially provided styles and meanings, and a '_____' which actively sought a minority style ...

a. Subculture
c. 28-hour day
b. 1990 Clean Air Act
d. 33 Strategies of War

11. _____, widely known as F. W. Taylor, was an American mechanical engineer who sought to improve industrial efficiency. He is regarded as the father of scientific management, and was one of the first management consultants.

Taylor was one of the intellectual leaders of the Efficiency Movement and his ideas, broadly conceived, were highly influential in the Progressive Era.

a. Douglas N. Daft
c. Geoffrey Colvin
b. Jonah Jacob Goldberg
d. Frederick Winslow Taylor

12. A _____ is a professional who provides advice in a particular area of expertise such as management, accountancy, the environment, entertainment, technology, law , human resources, marketing, medicine, finance, economics, public affairs, communication, engineering, sound system design, graphic design, or waste management.

A _____ is usually an expert or a professional in a specific field and has a wide knowledge of the subject matter. A _____ usually works for a consultancy firm or is self-employed, and engages with multiple and changing clients.

a. 1990 Clean Air Act
c. 33 Strategies of War
b. 28-hour day
d. Consultant

13. _____ refers to increasing the spiritual, political, social or economic strength of individuals and communities. It often involves the empowered developing confidence in their own capacities.

The term Human _____ covers a vast landscape of meanings, interpretations, definitions and disciplines ranging from psychology and philosophy to the highly commercialized Self-Help industry and Motivational sciences.

   a. A Stake in the Outcome
   c. AAAI
   b. Empowerment
   d. A4e

14. A _____ is a provisional group of workers who work for an organization on a non-permanent basis independent professionals, temporary contract workers, independent contractors or consultants. _____ Management is the strategic approach to managing an organization's _____ in a way that it reduces the company's cost in the management of contingent employees and mitigates the company's risk in employing them.

According to the US Bureau of Labor Statistics, the nontraditional workforce includes 'multiple job holders, contingent and part-time workers, and people in alternative work arrangements.' These workers currently represent a substantial portion of the U.S. workforce, and 'nearly four out of five employers, in establishments of all sizes and industries, use some form of nontraditional staffing.' 'People in alternative work arrangements' includes independent contractors, employees of contract companies, workers who are on call, and temporary workers.

   a. 33 Strategies of War
   c. 1990 Clean Air Act
   b. 28-hour day
   d. Contingent workforce

15. _____ has been described as the 'process of social influence in which one person can enlist the aid and support of others in the accomplishment of a common task' . A definition more inclusive of followers comes from Alan Keith of Genentech who said '_____ is ultimately about creating a way for people to contribute to making something extraordinary happen.'

_____ is one of the most salient aspects of the organizational context. However, defining _____ has been challenging.

   a. Leadership
   c. 1990 Clean Air Act
   b. 28-hour day
   d. Situational leadership

16. _____ is a layer of management in an organization whose primary job responsibility is to monitor activities of subordinates while reporting to upper management.

In pre-computer times, _____ would collect information from junior management and reassemble it for senior management. With the advent of inexpensive PCs this function has been taken over by e-business systems.

   a. Middle management
   c. Theory Y
   b. Community management
   d. Continuous monitoring

Chapter 5. The Manager's Environment

17. _____ is a management technique pioneered by Michael Phillips in San Francisco in the late '60's and early '70s. The concept's most visible success was by Jack Stack and his team at SRC Holdings and popularized in 1995 by John Case. The technique is to give employees all relevant financial information about the company so they can make better decisions as workers.

   a. AAAI
   b. A4e
   c. Open-book management
   d. A Stake in the Outcome

18. An _____ is a mostly hierarchical concept of subordination of entities that collaborate and contribute to serve one common aim.

Organizations are a variant of clustered entities. The structure of an organization is usually set up in many a styles, dependent on their objectives and ambience.

   a. Organizational structure
   b. Organizational development
   c. Open shop
   d. Informal organization

19. A _____ is a contemporary apporach to organizational design. It is an organization that is not defined by, or limited to, the horizontal, vertical, or external boundaries imposed by a predefined structure. This term was coined by former GE chairman Jack Welch because he wanted to eliminate vertical and horizontal boundaries within GE and break down external barriers between the company and its customers and suppliers.

   a. Chief risk officer
   b. Business Roundtable
   c. Headquarters
   d. Boundaryless organization

20. A _____ is a group of employees from various functional areas of the organization - research, engineering, marketing, finance. human resources, and operations, for example - who are all focused on a specific objective and are responsible to work as a team to improve coordination and innovation across divisions and resolve mutual problems.

   a. Sociotechnical systems
   b. Goal-setting theory
   c. Graduate recruitment
   d. Cross-functional team

21. _____ comprises a range of practices used in an organisation to identify, create, represent, distribute and enable adoption of insights and experiences. Such insights and experiences comprise knowledge, either embodied in individuals or embedded in organisational processes or practice.

An established discipline since 1991 , _____ includes courses taught in the fields of business administration, information systems, management, and library and information sciences .

   a. 1990 Clean Air Act
   b. Knowledge management
   c. 33 Strategies of War
   d. 28-hour day

22. A _____ is the term given to a company that facilitates the learning of its members and continuously transforms itself. _____s develop as a result of the pressures facing modern organizations and enables them to remain competitive in the business environment. A _____ has five main features; systems thinking, personal mastery, mental models, shared vision and team learning.

   a. Hoshin Kanri
   b. Quality function deployment
   c. Learning organization
   d. 1990 Clean Air Act

Chapter 5. The Manager's Environment

23. In economics, business, retail, and accounting, a _____ is the value of money that has been used up to produce something, and hence is not available for use anymore. In economics, a _____ is an alternative that is given up as a result of a decision. In business, the _____ may be one of acquisition, in which case the amount of money expended to acquire it is counted as _____.
   a. Cost allocation
   b. Fixed costs
   c. Cost overrun
   d. Cost

24. The _____ was a period in the late 18th and early 19th centuries when major changes in agriculture, manufacturing, mining, and transportation had a profound effect on the socioeconomic and cultural conditions in Britain. The changes subsequently spread throughout Europe, North America, and eventually the world. The onset of the _____ marked a major turning point in human society; almost every aspect of daily life was eventually influenced in some way.
   a. Industrial Revolution
   b. Adam Smith
   c. Abraham Harold Maslow
   d. Affiliation

25. _____ is the state or fact of exclusive rights and control over property, which may be an object, land/real estate or intellectual property. An _____ right is also referred to as title. The concept of _____ has existed for thousands of years and in all cultures.
   a. Ownership
   b. A4e
   c. Emanation of the state
   d. A Stake in the Outcome

26. In economics, and cost accounting, _____ describes the total economic cost of production and is made up of variable costs, which vary according to the quantity of a good produced and include inputs such as labor and raw materials, plus fixed costs, which are independent of the quantity of a good produced and include inputs (capital) that cannot be varied in the short term, such as buildings and machinery. _____ in economics includes the total opportunity cost of each factor of production in addition to fixed and variable costs.

The rate at which _____ changes as the amount produced changes is called marginal cost.

   a. 1990 Clean Air Act
   b. 28-hour day
   c. 33 Strategies of War
   d. Total Cost

27. _____ is a financial estimate designed to help consumers and enterprise managers assess direct and indirect costs It is a form of full cost accounting.
   a. 1990 Clean Air Act
   b. 28-hour day
   c. 33 Strategies of War
   d. Total Cost of Ownership

28. _____ is a technical term used in management science popularized by Joseph M. Juran

He defined an internal and external customers as anyone affected by the product or by the process used to produce the product, in the context of quality management. _____s may play the role as supplier, processer, and customer in the sequence of product development.

He claimed that the organization must understand and identify both internal and external customers and their needs.

a. A4e
b. A Stake in the Outcome
c. AAAI
d. Internal customer

29. In economics, the people in the _____ are the suppliers of labor. The _____ is all the nonmilitary people who are employed or unemployed. In 2005, the worldwide _____ was over 3 billion people.
   a. Pink-collar worker
   b. Decent work
   c. Departmentalization
   d. Labor force

30. _____ generally refers to a list of all planned expenses and revenues. It is a plan for saving and spending. A _____ is an important concept in microeconomics, which uses a _____ line to illustrate the trade-offs between two or more goods.
   a. Budget
   b. 33 Strategies of War
   c. 1990 Clean Air Act
   d. 28-hour day

31. A _____ is a customs union with common policies on product regulation, and freedom of movement of the factors of production (capital and labour) and of enterprise. The goal is that the movement of capital, labour, goods, and services between the members is as easy as within them. This is the fourth stage of economic integration.
   a. Trade creation
   b. Common Market
   c. Most favoured nation
   d. Trade barrier

32. In game theory, an _____ is a set of moves or strategies taken by the players, or their payoffs resulting from the actions or strategies taken by all players. The two are complementary in that given knowledge of the set of strategies of all players, the final state of the game is known, as are any relevant payoffs. In a game where chance or a random event is involved, the _____ is not known from only the set of strategies, but is only realized when the random event(s) are realized.
   a. AAAI
   b. Outcome
   c. A4e
   d. A Stake in the Outcome

33. A _____ is a type of business entity in which partners (owners) share with each other the profits or losses of the business. _____s are often favored over corporations for taxation purposes, as the _____ structure does not generally incur a tax on profits before it is distributed to the partners (i.e. there is no dividend tax levied.) However, depending on the _____ structure and the jurisdiction in which it operates, owners of a _____ may be exposed to greater personal liability than they would as shareholders of a corporation.
   a. Mediation
   b. Due process
   c. Partnership
   d. Federal Employers Liability Act

34. A _____ also known as a sole trader, or simply proprietorship is a type of business entity which there is only one owner and he has the final word taking all desicions by himself. All debts of the business are debts of the owner and must pay from his personal possessions. This means that the owner has unlimited liabilty.
   a. Foreign ownership
   b. Sole proprietorship
   c. Business rule
   d. Golden hello

35. An _____ is a private computer network that uses Internet technologies to securely share any part of an organization's information or operational systems with its employees. Sometimes the term refers only to the organization's internal website, but often it is a more extensive part of the organization's computer infrastructure and private websites are an important component and focal point of internal communication and collaboration.

An _____ is built from the same concepts and technologies used for the Internet, such as client-server computing and the Internet Protocol Suite (TCP/IP.)

a. AAAI
b. A4e
c. A Stake in the Outcome
d. Intranet

Chapter 6. Organizational Planning

1. _____ is the process of recruiting individuals to fill executive positions in organizations. _____ may be performed by an organization's board of directors, by executives in the organization, or by an outside _____ organization.

The _____ profession has two distinct fields, retained _____ and contingency search.

   a. Employee referral   b. Executive Search
   c. Employment agency   d. Internet recruiting

2. _____, commonly known as e-commerce, consists of the buying and selling of products or services over electronic systems such as the Internet and other computer networks. The amount of trade conducted electronically has grown extraordinarily with widespread Internet usage. The use of commerce is conducted in this way, spurring and drawing on innovations in electronic funds transfer, supply chain management, Internet marketing, online transaction processing, electronic data interchange (EDI), inventory management systems, and automated data collection systems.

   a. Electronic commerce   b. A Stake in the Outcome
   c. A4e   d. Online shopping

3. A _____ is a brief written statement of the purpose of a company or organization. Ideally, a _____ guides the actions of the organization, spells out its overall goal, provides a sense of direction, and guides decision making for all levels of management.

_____s often contain the following:

- Purpose and aim of the organization
- The organization's primary stakeholders: clients, stockholders, etc.
- Responsibilities of the organization toward these stakeholders
- Products and services offered

In developing a _____:

- Encourage as much input as feasible from employees, volunteers, and other stakeholders
- Publicize it broadly

The _____ can be used to resolve differences between business stakeholders. Stakeholders include: employees including managers and executives, stockholders, board of directors, customers, suppliers, distributors, creditors, governments (local, state, federal, etc.), unions, competitors, NGO's, and the general public.

   a. 28-hour day   b. 33 Strategies of War
   c. 1990 Clean Air Act   d. Mission statement

4. _____ was a writer, management consultant, and self-described 'social ecologist.' Widely considered to be 'the father of modern management,' his 39 books and countless scholarly and popular articles explored how humans are organized across all sectors of society--in business, government and the nonprofit world. His writings have predicted many of the major developments of the late twentieth century, including privatization and decentralization; the rise of Japan to economic world power; the decisive importance of marketing; and the emergence of the information society with its necessity of lifelong learning. In 1959, Drucker coined the term 'knowledge worker' and later in his life considered knowledge work productivity to be the next frontier of management.

Chapter 6. Organizational Planning

a. Peter Ferdinand Drucker
b. Jacques Al-Salawat Nasruddin Nasser
c. Debora L. Spar
d. Chrissie Hynde

5. _____ is a term used in general business practice to describe methodologies, systems, and practices designed to generate new potential business clientele, generally operated through a variety of marketing techniques. _____ facilitates a business's connection between its outgoing consumer advertising and the responses to that advertising. These processes are designed for business-to-business and direct-to-consumer strategies.

a. Lead Management
b. Lead generation
c. 1990 Clean Air Act
d. Request for Proposal

6. _____ refers to both the industry of, and the practice of, helping organizations improve their performance, primarily through the analysis of existing business problems and development of plans for improvement.

Organizations hire the services of management consultants for a number of reasons, including gaining external (and presumably objective) advice, access to the consultants' specialized expertise, or simply as extra temporary help during a one-time project, where the hiring of more permanent employees is not required.

Because of their exposure to and relationships with numerous organizations, consultancies are also said to be aware of industry 'best practices', although the transferability of such practices from one organization to another is the subject of debate.

a. 28-hour day
b. 1990 Clean Air Act
c. 33 Strategies of War
d. Management Consulting

7. _____ is a layer of management in an organization whose primary job responsibility is to monitor activities of subordinates while reporting to upper management.

In pre-computer times, _____ would collect information from junior management and reassemble it for senior management. With the advent of inexpensive PCs this function has been taken over by e-business systems.

a. Community management
b. Theory Y
c. Continuous monitoring
d. Middle management

8. The 'business case for _____', theorizes that in a global marketplace, a company that employs a diverse workforce (both men and women, people of many generations, people from ethnically and racially diverse backgrounds etc.) is better able to understand the demographics of the marketplace it serves and is thus better equipped to thrive in that marketplace than a company that has a more limited range of employee demographics.

An additional corollary suggests that a company that supports the _____ of its workforce can also improve employee satisfaction, productivity and retention.

a. Trademark
b. Kanban
c. Virtual team
d. Diversity

9. _____ refers to increasing the spiritual, political, social or economic strength of individuals and communities. It often involves the empowered developing confidence in their own capacities.

The term Human _____ covers a vast landscape of meanings, interpretations, definitions and disciplines ranging from psychology and philosophy to the highly commercialized Self-Help industry and Motivational sciences.

a. Empowerment
b. AAAI
c. A Stake in the Outcome
d. A4e

10. _____ is a contract between two parties, one being the employer and the other being the employee. An employee may be defined as: 'A person in the service of another under any contract of hire, express or implied, oral or written, where the employer has the power or right to control and direct the employee in the material details of how the work is to be performed.' Black's Law Dictionary page 471 (5th ed. 1979.)

a. Employment rate
b. Exit interview
c. Employment counsellor
d. Employment

11. The term _____ was created by President Lyndon B. Johnson when he signed Executive Order 11246 on September 24, 1965, created to prohibit federal contractors from discriminating against employees on the basis of race, sex, creed, religion, color, or national origin. In more recent times, most employers have also added sexual orientation to the list of non-discrimination.

The Executive Order also required contractors to implement affirmative action plans to increase the participation of minorities and women in the workplace.

a. A4e
b. A Stake in the Outcome
c. AAAI
d. Equal Employment Opportunity

12. The U.S. _____ is a federal agency whose goal is ending employment discrimination. The _____ investigates discrimination complaints based on an individual's race, color, national origin, religion, sex, age, disability and retaliation for reporting and/or opposing a discriminatory practice. The Commission is also tasked with filing suits on behalf of alleged victim(s) of discrimination against employers and as an adjudicatory for claims of discrimination brought against federal agencies.

a. ARCO
b. Airbus SAS
c. Equal Employment Opportunity Commission
d. Airbus Industrie

13. In game theory, an _____ is a set of moves or strategies taken by the players, or their payoffs resulting from the actions or strategies taken by all players. The two are complementary in that given knowledge of the set of strategies of all players, the final state of the game is known, as are any relevant payoffs. In a game where chance or a random event is involved, the _____ is not known from only the set of strategies, but is only realized when the random event(s) are realized.

a. Outcome
b. A Stake in the Outcome
c. A4e
d. AAAI

Chapter 6. Organizational Planning

14. Procter is a surname, and may also refer to:

- Bryan Waller Procter (pseud. Barry Cornwall), English poet
- Goodwin Procter, American law firm
- _____, consumer products multinational

    a. Downstream
    b. Strict liability
    c. Master and Servant Acts
    d. Procter ' Gamble

15. _____ is a Fortune 500, American multinational corporation headquartered in Cincinnati, Ohio, that manufactures a wide range of consumer goods. As of 2008, P'G is the 8th largest corporation in the world by market capitalization and 14th largest US company by profit.

    a. Turnover
    b. Maturity of Organizations and Business Excellence - The Four-Phase Model
    c. STAR
    d. Procter ' Gamble Co.

16. _____ generally refers to a list of all planned expenses and revenues. It is a plan for saving and spending. A _____ is an important concept in microeconomics, which uses a _____ line to illustrate the trade-offs between two or more goods.

    a. Budget
    b. 28-hour day
    c. 33 Strategies of War
    d. 1990 Clean Air Act

17. A _____ is typically described as a deliberate plan of action to guide decisions and achieve rational outcome(s.) However, the term may also be used to denote what is actually done, even though it is unplanned.

The term may apply to government, private sector organizations and groups, and individuals.

    a. 28-hour day
    b. Policy
    c. 33 Strategies of War
    d. 1990 Clean Air Act

18. The _____, 5 U.S.C. § 552a, establishes a code of fair information practices that governs the collection, maintenance, use, and dissemination of personally identifiable information about individuals that is maintained in systems of records by federal agencies. A system of records is a group of records under the control of an agency from which information is retrieved by the name of the individual or by some identifier assigned to the individual.

    a. Negligence
    b. Privacy Act of 1974
    c. Personal Responsibility and Work Opportunity Reconciliation Act
    d. No-FEAR Act

19. A _____ is a plan devised for a specific situation when things could go wrong. _____s are often devised by governments or businesses who want to be prepared for anything that could happen. They are sometimes known as 'Back-up plans', 'Worst-case scenario plans' or 'Plan B'.

    a. 28-hour day
    b. 1990 Clean Air Act
    c. 33 Strategies of War
    d. Contingency plan

Chapter 6. Organizational Planning

20. _____ is a broad label that refers to any individuals or households that use goods and services generated within the economy. The concept of a _____ is used in different contexts, so that the usage and significance of the term may vary.

Typically when business people and economists talk of _____s they are talking about person as _____, an aggregated commodity item with little individuality other than that expressed in the buy/not-buy decision.

- a. 33 Strategies of War
- b. Consumer
- c. 1990 Clean Air Act
- d. 28-hour day

21. _____ is the process of estimation in unknown situations. Prediction is a similar, but more general term. Both can refer to estimation of time series, cross-sectional or longitudinal data.
- a. 33 Strategies of War
- b. 1990 Clean Air Act
- c. Forecasting
- d. 28-hour day

22. In mathematics, _____ is a technique for optimization of a linear objective function, subject to linear equality and linear inequality constraints. Informally, _____ determines the way to achieve the best outcome (such as maximum profit or lowest cost) in a given mathematical model and given some list of requirements represented as linear equations.

More formally, given a polytope (for example, a polygon or a polyhedron), and a real-valued affine function

$$f(x_1, x_2, \ldots, x_n) = c_1 x_1 + c_2 x_2 + \cdots + c_n x_n + d$$

defined on this polytope, a _____ method will find a point in the polytope where this function has the smallest (or largest) value.

- a. 1990 Clean Air Act
- b. Slack variable
- c. Linear programming relaxation
- d. Linear programming

23. The _____ captures an expanded spectrum of values and criteria for measuring organizational success: economic, ecological and social. With the ratification of the United Nations and ICLEI _____ standard for urban and community accounting in early 2007, this became the dominant approach to public sector full cost accounting. Similar UN standards apply to natural capital and human capital measurement to assist in measurements required by _____, e.g. the ecoBudget standard for reporting ecological footprint.
- a. 28-hour day
- b. 33 Strategies of War
- c. 1990 Clean Air Act
- d. Triple bottom line

Chapter 7. Strategic Planning and Strategic Management

1. _____ is an organization's process of defining its strategy and making decisions on allocating its resources to pursue this strategy, including its capital and people. Various business analysis techniques can be used in _____, including SWOT analysis (Strengths, Weaknesses, Opportunities, and Threats) and PEST analysis (Political, Economic, Social, and Technological analysis) or STEER analysis involving Socio-cultural, Technological, Economic, Ecological, and Regulatory factors and EPISTEL (Environment, Political, Informatic, Social, Technological, Economic and Legal)

_____ is the formal consideration of an organization's future course. All _____ deals with at least one of three key questions:

1. 'What do we do?'
2. 'For whom do we do it?'
3. 'How do we excel?'

In business _____, the third question is better phrased 'How can we beat or avoid competition?'. (Bradford and Duncan, page 1.)

a. 33 Strategies of War
b. 1990 Clean Air Act
c. 28-hour day
d. Strategic planning

2. _____ is, in very basic words, a position a firm occupies against its competitors.

According to Michael Porter, the three methods for creating a sustainable _____ are through:

1. Cost leadership

2. Differentiation

3. Focus (economics)

a. Competitive advantage
b. 28-hour day
c. 1990 Clean Air Act
d. Theory Z

3. _____ is a strategic planning method used to evaluate the Strengths, Weaknesses, Opportunities, and Threats involved in a project or in a business venture. It involves specifying the objective of the business venture or project and identifying the internal and external factors that are favorable and unfavorable to achieving that objective. The technique is credited to Albert Humphrey, who led a convention at Stanford University in the 1960s and 1970s using data from Fortune 500 companies.

a. SWOT analysis
b. Market share
c. Marketing
d. Corporate image

4. _____ is the term used to describe a situation where different entities cooperate advantageously for a final outcome. Simply defined, it means that the whole is greater than the sum of the individual parts. Although the whole will be greater than each individual part, this is not the concept of _____.

a. 33 Strategies of War
b. 1990 Clean Air Act
c. 28-hour day
d. Synergy

Chapter 7. Strategic Planning and Strategic Management

5. _____ is a recursive process where two or more people or organizations work together in an intersection of common goals -- for example, an intellectual endeavor that is creative in nature--by sharing knowledge, learning and building consensus. _____ does not require leadership and can sometimes bring better results through decentralization and egalitarianism. In particular, teams that work collaboratively can obtain greater resources, recognition and reward when facing competition for finite resources._____ is also present in opposing goals exhibiting the notion of adversarial _____, though this is not a common case for using the term.

   a. Collectivism
   c. Collaboration
   b. 1990 Clean Air Act
   d. 28-hour day

6. A _____ is a plan devised for a specific situation when things could go wrong. _____s are often devised by governments or businesses who want to be prepared for anything that could happen. They are sometimes known as 'Back-up plans', 'Worst-case scenario plans' or 'Plan B'.

   a. 1990 Clean Air Act
   c. Contingency plan
   b. 33 Strategies of War
   d. 28-hour day

7. Organizational culture is not the same as _____. It is wider and deeper concepts, something that an organization 'is' rather than what it 'has' (according to Buchanan and Huczynski.)

   _____ is the total sum of the values, customs, traditions and meanings that make a company unique.

   a. Path-goal theory
   c. Work design
   b. Job analysis
   d. Corporate Culture

8. _____ is the process of recruiting individuals to fill executive positions in organizations. _____ may be performed by an organization's board of directors, by executives in the organization, or by an outside _____ organization.

   The _____ profession has two distinct fields, retained _____ and contingency search.

   a. Employment agency
   c. Internet recruiting
   b. Executive Search
   d. Employee referral

9. _____ is a term used in general business practice to describe methodologies, systems, and practices designed to generate new potential business clientele, generally operated through a variety of marketing techniques. _____ facilitates a business's connection between its outgoing consumer advertising and the responses to that advertising. These processes are designed for business-to-business and direct-to-consumer strategies.

   a. Lead Management
   c. 1990 Clean Air Act
   b. Lead generation
   d. Request for Proposal

10. _____ refers to both the industry of, and the practice of, helping organizations improve their performance, primarily through the analysis of existing business problems and development of plans for improvement.

Organizations hire the services of management consultants for a number of reasons, including gaining external (and presumably objective) advice, access to the consultants' specialized expertise, or simply as extra temporary help during a one-time project, where the hiring of more permanent employees is not required.

Chapter 7. Strategic Planning and Strategic Management

Because of their exposure to and relationships with numerous organizations, consultancies are also said to be aware of industry 'best practices', although the transferability of such practices from one organization to another is the subject of debate.

a. Management Consulting
b. 1990 Clean Air Act
c. 33 Strategies of War
d. 28-hour day

11. A _____ is a brief written statement of the purpose of a company or organization. Ideally, a _____ guides the actions of the organization, spells out its overall goal, provides a sense of direction, and guides decision making for all levels of management.

_____s often contain the following:

- Purpose and aim of the organization
- The organization's primary stakeholders: clients, stockholders, etc.
- Responsibilities of the organization toward these stakeholders
- Products and services offered

In developing a _____:

- Encourage as much input as feasible from employees, volunteers, and other stakeholders
- Publicize it broadly

The _____ can be used to resolve differences between business stakeholders. Stakeholders include: employees including managers and executives, stockholders, board of directors, customers, suppliers, distributors, creditors, governments (local, state, federal, etc.), unions, competitors, NGO's, and the general public.

a. 1990 Clean Air Act
b. 33 Strategies of War
c. 28-hour day
d. Mission statement

12. A _____ is a professional who provides advice in a particular area of expertise such as management, accountancy, the environment, entertainment, technology, law, human resources, marketing, medicine, finance, economics, public affairs, communication, engineering, sound system design, graphic design, or waste management.

A _____ is usually an expert or a professional in a specific field and has a wide knowledge of the subject matter. A _____ usually works for a consultancy firm or is self-employed, and engages with multiple and changing clients.

a. 1990 Clean Air Act
b. 28-hour day
c. 33 Strategies of War
d. Consultant

13. _____ is something that a firm can do well and that meets the following three conditions:

Chapter 7. Strategic Planning and Strategic Management

Competencies are things that companys execute well across several business units or product sectors.

Firms usually have few competencies, but these are usually less liable to change rapidly.

1. It provides consumer benefits
2. It is not easy for competitors to imitate
3. It can be leveraged widely to many products and markets.

A _____ can take various forms, including technical/subject matter know-how, a reliable process and/or close relationships with customers and suppliers (Mascarenhas et al. 1998.)

  a. Learning-by-doing
  b. NAIRU
  c. Dominant Design
  d. Core competency

14. The term _____ collectively refers to all resources that determine the value and the competitiveness of an enterprise. As such, it includes as subsets the attributes that concur to building all financial statements as well as the balance sheet.
  a. A Stake in the Outcome
  b. Intellectual capital
  c. AAAI
  d. A4e

15. _____ is a form of corporate self-regulation integrated into a business model. Ideally, _____ policy would function as a built-in, self-regulating mechanism whereby business would monitor and ensure their adherence to law, ethical standards, and international norms. Business would embrace responsibility for the impact of their activities on the environment, consumers, employees, communities, stakeholders and all other members of the public sphere.
  a. Corporate social responsibility
  b. 33 Strategies of War
  c. 1990 Clean Air Act
  d. 28-hour day

16. _____ is an increasingly broadening term with which an organization, or other human system describes the combination of traditionally administrative personnel functions with acquisition and application of skills, knowledge and experience, Employee Relations and resource planning at various levels. The field draws upon concepts developed in Industrial/Organizational Psychology and System Theory. _____ has at least two related interpretations depending on context. The original usage derives from political economy and economics, where it was traditionally called labor, one of four factors of production although this perspective is changing as a function of new and ongoing research into more strategic approaches at national levels. This first usage is used more in terms of '_____ development', and can go beyond just organizations to the level of nations . The more traditional usage within corporations and businesses refers to the individuals within a firm or agency, and to the portion of the organization that deals with hiring, firing, training, and other personnel issues, typically referred to as `_____ management'.
  a. Human resource management
  b. Progressive discipline
  c. Human resources
  d. Bradford Factor

17. An _____ is a mostly hierarchical concept of subordination of entities that collaborate and contribute to serve one common aim.

Organizations are a variant of clustered entities. The structure of an organization is usually set up in many a styles, dependent on their objectives and ambience.

Chapter 7. Strategic Planning and Strategic Management

a. Organizational structure
b. Open shop
c. Informal organization
d. Organizational development

18. _____ is a form of communication that typically attempts to persuade potential customers to purchase or to consume more of a particular brand of product or service. 'While now central to the contemporary global economy and the reproduction of global production networks, it is only quite recently that _____ has been more than a marginal influence on patterns of sales and production. The formation of modern _____ was intimately bound up with the emergence of new forms of monopoly capitalism around the end of the 19th and beginning of the 20th century as one element in corporate strategies to create, organize and where possible control markets, especially for mass produced consumer goods.

a. Advertising
b. AAAI
c. A Stake in the Outcome
d. A4e

19. In microeconomics and strategic management, the term _____ describes a type of ownership and control. It is a strategy used by a business or corporation that seeks to sell a type of product in numerous markets. _____ in marketing is much more common than vertical integration is in production.

a. Career development
b. Farmshoring
c. No-bid contract
d. Horizontal integration

20. In microeconomics and management, the term _____ describes a style of management control. Vertically integrated companies are united through a hierarchy with a common owner. Usually each member of the hierarchy produces a different product or (market-specific) service, and the products combine to satisfy a common need.

a. 28-hour day
b. 33 Strategies of War
c. 1990 Clean Air Act
d. Vertical integration

21. A _____ is a name or trademark connected with a product or producer. _____s have become increasingly important components of culture and the economy, now being described as 'cultural accessories and personal philosophies'.

Some people distinguish the psychological aspect of a _____ from the experiential aspect.

a. Brand
b. Brand awareness
c. Brand extension
d. Brand loyalty

22. _____ is understood as a business unit within the overall corporate identity which is distinguishable from other business because it serves a defined external market where management can conduct strategic planning in relation to products and markets. When companies become really large, they are best thought of as being composed of a number of businesses (or _____s.)

In the broader domain of strategic management, the phrase '_____' came into use in the 1960s, largely as a result of General Electric's many units.

a. Switching cost
b. Strategic business unit
c. Strategic drift
d. Strategic group

23. _____ is the largest book retailer in the United States, operating mainly through its Barnes ' Noble Booksellers chain of bookstores headquartered in lower Fifth Avenue in Manhattan.

Chapter 7. Strategic Planning and Strategic Management

The company operates the chain of small 'B.

- a. 33 Strategies of War
- b. 28-hour day
- c. 1990 Clean Air Act
- d. Barnes ' Noble, Inc.

24. _____ (NYSE: DE) is an American corporation based in Moline, Illinois, and the leading manufacturer of agricultural machinery in the world. In 2008, it was listed as 102nd in the Fortune 500 ranking. Deere and Company agricultural products, usually sold under the John Deere name, include tractors, combine harvesters, balers, planters/seeders, ATVs and forestry equipment.

- a. 28-hour day
- b. 33 Strategies of War
- c. 1990 Clean Air Act
- d. Deere ' Company

25. _____ is a form of applied ethics that examines ethical principles and moral or ethical problems that arise in a business environment. It applies to all aspects of business conduct and is relevant to the conduct of individuals and business organizations as a whole. Applied ethics is a field of ethics that deals with ethical questions in many fields such as medical, technical, legal and _____.

- a. Hypernorms
- b. Corporate Sustainability
- c. Business Ethics
- d. Facilitation payments

26. Procter is a surname, and may also refer to:

- Bryan Waller Procter (pseud. Barry Cornwall), English poet
- Goodwin Procter, American law firm
- _____, consumer products multinational

- a. Strict liability
- b. Downstream
- c. Master and Servant Acts
- d. Procter ' Gamble

27. _____ is a Fortune 500, American multinational corporation headquartered in Cincinnati, Ohio, that manufactures a wide range of consumer goods. As of 2008, P'G is the 8th largest corporation in the world by market capitalization and 14th largest US company by profit.

- a. Procter ' Gamble Co.
- b. Maturity of Organizations and Business Excellence - The Four-Phase Model
- c. STAR
- d. Turnover

28. The 'business case for _____', theorizes that in a global marketplace, a company that employs a diverse workforce (both men and women, people of many generations, people from ethnically and racially diverse backgrounds etc.) is better able to understand the demographics of the marketplace it serves and is thus better equipped to thrive in that marketplace than a company that has a more limited range of employee demographics.

An additional corollary suggests that a company that supports the _____ of its workforce can also improve employee satisfaction, productivity and retention.

a. Virtual team b. Trademark
c. Kanban d. Diversity

29. _____ is an integrated communications-based process through which individuals and communities discover that existing and newly-identified needs and wants may be satisfied by the products and services of others.

_____ is defined by the American _____ Association as the activity, set of institutions, and processes for creating, communicating, delivering, and exchanging offerings that have value for customers, clients, partners, and society at large. The term developed from the original meaning which referred literally to going to market, as in shopping, or going to a market to buy or sell goods or services.

a. Disruptive technology b. Marketing
c. Customer relationship management d. Market development

30. _____ is a form of marketing developed from direct response marketing campaigns conducted in the 1970s and 1980s which emphasizes customer retention and satisfaction, rather than a dominant focus on point-of-sale transactions.

_____ differs from other forms of marketing in that it recognizes the long term value to the firm of keeping customers, as opposed to direct or 'Intrusion' marketing, which focuses upon acquisition of new clients by targeting majority demographics based upon prospective client lists.

_____ refers to a long-term and mutually beneficial arrangement wherein both the buyer and seller focus on value enhancement with the goal of providing a more satisfying exchange.

a. Relationship Marketing b. 1990 Clean Air Act
c. Guerrilla marketing d. 28-hour day

31. _____ refers to the aggregated strategies of single business firm or a strategic business unit (SBU) in a diversified corporation. According to Michael Porter, a firm must formulate a _____ that incorporates either cost leadership, differentiation or focus in order to achieve a sustainable competitive advantage and long-term success in its chosen arenas or industries.

Functional strategies include marketing strategies, new product development strategies, human resource strategies, financial strategies, legal strategies, supply-chain strategies, and information technology management strategies.

a. Competitive heterogeneity b. Switching cost
c. Business strategy d. Strategic thinking

32. The phrase _____, according to the Organization for Economic Co-operation and Development, refers to 'creative work undertaken on a systematic basis in order to increase the stock of knowledge, including knowledge of man, culture and society, and the use of this stock of knowledge to devise new applications [sic]'

Chapter 7. Strategic Planning and Strategic Management

New product design and development is more than often a crucial factor in the survival of a company. In an industry that is fast changing, firms must continually revise their design and range of products. This is necessary due to continuous technology change and development as well as other competitors and the changing preference of customers.

a. Research and development
c. 1990 Clean Air Act
b. 33 Strategies of War
d. 28-hour day

33. The _____ is given by the United States National Institute of Standards and Technology. Through the actions of the National Productivity Advisory Committee chaired by Jack Grayson, it was established by the Malcolm Baldrige National Quality Improvement Act of 1987 - Public Law 100-107 and named for Malcolm Baldrige, who served as United States Secretary of Commerce during the Reagan administration from 1981 until his 1987 death in a rodeo accident. APQC, , organized the first White House Conference on Productivity, spearheading the creation and design of the _____ in 1987, and jointly administering the award for its first three years.

a. Time and attendance
c. Scenario planning
b. Malcolm Baldrige National Quality Award
d. Business Network Transformation

Chapter 8. Making Decisions

1. A _____ is a brief written statement of the purpose of a company or organization. Ideally, a _____ guides the actions of the organization, spells out its overall goal, provides a sense of direction, and guides decision making for all levels of management.

_____s often contain the following:

- Purpose and aim of the organization
- The organization's primary stakeholders: clients, stockholders, etc.
- Responsibilities of the organization toward these stakeholders
- Products and services offered

In developing a _____:

- Encourage as much input as feasible from employees, volunteers, and other stakeholders
- Publicize it broadly

The _____ can be used to resolve differences between business stakeholders. Stakeholders include: employees including managers and executives, stockholders, board of directors, customers, suppliers, distributors, creditors, governments (local, state, federal, etc.), unions, competitors, NGO's, and the general public.

    a. 1990 Clean Air Act   b. 33 Strategies of War
    c. 28-hour day   d. Mission statement

2. _____ can be regarded as an outcome of mental processes (cognitive process) leading to the selection of a course of action among several alternatives. Every _____ process produces a final choice. The output can be an action or an opinion of choice.

    a. 28-hour day   b. 33 Strategies of War
    c. Decision making   d. 1990 Clean Air Act

3. _____ is one of the managerial functions like planning, organizing, staffing and directing. It is an important function because it helps to check the errors and to take the corrective action so that deviation from standards are minimized and stated goals of the organization are achieved in desired manner. According to modern concepts, _____ is a foreseeing action whereas earlier concept of _____ was used only when errors were detected. _____ in management means setting standards, measuring actual performance and taking corrective action.

    a. Decision tree pruning   b. Turnover
    c. Schedule of reinforcement   d. Control

4. _____ has been described as the 'process of social influence in which one person can enlist the aid and support of others in the accomplishment of a common task' . A definition more inclusive of followers comes from Alan Keith of Genentech who said '_____ is ultimately about creating a way for people to contribute to making something extraordinary happen.'

_____ is one of the most salient aspects of the organizational context. However, defining _____ has been challenging.

Chapter 8. Making Decisions

   a. 1990 Clean Air Act
   b. 28-hour day
   c. Situational leadership
   d. Leadership

5. The _____, 5 U.S.C. § 552a, establishes a code of fair information practices that governs the collection, maintenance, use, and dissemination of personally identifiable information about individuals that is maintained in systems of records by federal agencies. A system of records is a group of records under the control of an agency from which information is retrieved by the name of the individual or by some identifier assigned to the individual.

   a. Personal Responsibility and Work Opportunity Reconciliation Act
   b. No-FEAR Act
   c. Negligence
   d. Privacy Act of 1974

6. _____, commonly known as e-commerce, consists of the buying and selling of products or services over electronic systems such as the Internet and other computer networks. The amount of trade conducted electronically has grown extraordinarily with widespread Internet usage. The use of commerce is conducted in this way, spurring and drawing on innovations in electronic funds transfer, supply chain management, Internet marketing, online transaction processing, electronic data interchange (EDI), inventory management systems, and automated data collection systems.

   a. A Stake in the Outcome
   b. Electronic commerce
   c. Online shopping
   d. A4e

7. A _____ is a list of the general tasks and responsibilities of a position. Typically, it also includes to whom the position reports, specifications such as the qualifications needed by the person in the job, salary range for the position, etc. A _____ is usually developed by conducting a job analysis, which includes examining the tasks and sequences of tasks necessary to perform the job.

   a. Recruitment advertising
   b. Recruitment
   c. Recruitment Process Insourcing
   d. Job description

8. Procter is a surname, and may also refer to:

   - Bryan Waller Procter (pseud. Barry Cornwall), English poet
   - Goodwin Procter, American law firm
   - _____, consumer products multinational

   a. Master and Servant Acts
   b. Downstream
   c. Procter ' Gamble
   d. Strict liability

9. _____ is a Fortune 500, American multinational corporation headquartered in Cincinnati, Ohio, that manufactures a wide range of consumer goods. As of 2008, P'G is the 8th largest corporation in the world by market capitalization and 14th largest US company by profit.

   a. STAR
   b. Procter ' Gamble Co.
   c. Maturity of Organizations and Business Excellence - The Four-Phase Model
   d. Turnover

10. _____ is a layer of management in an organization whose primary job responsibility is to monitor activities of subordinates while reporting to upper management.

In pre-computer times, _____ would collect information from junior management and reassemble it for senior management. With the advent of inexpensive PCs this function has been taken over by e-business systems.

a. Theory Y
b. Community management
c. Continuous monitoring
d. Middle management

11. The U.S. _____ is an independent agency of the United States government which holds primary responsibility for enforcing the federal securities laws and regulating the securities industry, the nation's stock and options exchanges, and other electronic securities markets. The SEC was created by section 4 of the Securities Exchange Act of 1934 (now codified as 15 U.S.C. § 78d and commonly referred to as the 1934 Act.)

a. 28-hour day
b. 33 Strategies of War
c. Securities and Exchange Commission
d. 1990 Clean Air Act

12. _____ was a writer, management consultant, and self-described 'social ecologist.' Widely considered to be 'the father of modern management,' his 39 books and countless scholarly and popular articles explored how humans are organized across all sectors of society--in business, government and the nonprofit world. His writings have predicted many of the major developments of the late twentieth century, including privatization and decentralization; the rise of Japan to economic world power; the decisive importance of marketing; and the emergence of the information society with its necessity of lifelong learning. In 1959, Drucker coined the term 'knowledge worker' and later in his life considered knowledge work productivity to be the next frontier of management.

a. Debora L. Spar
b. Jacques Al-Salawat Nasruddin Nasser
c. Chrissie Hynde
d. Peter Ferdinand Drucker

13. _____ is an American writer on business management practices, best-known for, In Search of Excellence (co-authored with Robert H. Waterman, Jr.)

Peters was born in Baltimore, Maryland. He went to Severn School for High School and attended Cornell University, receiving a bachelor's degree in civil engineering in 1965, and a master's degree in 1966.

a. Affiliation
b. Abraham Harold Maslow
c. Thomas J. Peters
d. Adam Smith

14. _____ is a strategic planning method used to evaluate the Strengths, Weaknesses, Opportunities, and Threats involved in a project or in a business venture. It involves specifying the objective of the business venture or project and identifying the internal and external factors that are favorable and unfavorable to achieving that objective. The technique is credited to Albert Humphrey, who led a convention at Stanford University in the 1960s and 1970s using data from Fortune 500 companies.

a. Market share
b. Corporate image
c. SWOT analysis
d. Marketing

15. Business-to-consumer describes activities of businesses serving end consumers with products and/or services.

An example of a _____ transaction would be a person buying a pair of shoes from a retailer. The transactions that led to the shoes being available for purchase, that is the purchase of the leather, laces, rubber, etc.

Chapter 8. Making Decisions

a. B2C
b. PEST analysis
c. Green marketing
d. Market environment

16. _____ consists of the sale of goods or merchandise from a fixed location, such as a department store, boutique or kiosk in small or individual lots for direct consumption by the purchaser. _____ may include subordinated services, such as delivery. Purchasers may be individuals or businesses.
    a. Planogram
    b. 28-hour day
    c. 1990 Clean Air Act
    d. Retailing

17. _____ describes the situation when output from (or information about the result of) an event or phenomenon in the past will influence the same event/phenomenon in the present or future. When an event is part of a chain of cause-and-effect that forms a circuit or loop, then the event is said to 'feed back' into itself.

_____ is also a synonym for:

- _____ signal; the information about the initial event that is the basis for subsequent modification of the event.
- _____ loop; the causal path that leads from the initial generation of the _____ signal to the subsequent modification of the event.

_____ is a mechanism, process or signal that is looped back to control a system within itself. Such a loop is called a _____ loop.

a. Feedback loop
b. 1990 Clean Air Act
c. Positive feedback
d. Feedback

18. In decision theory and estimation theory, the _____ of an estimator, $\hat{\theta}$, of an unknown parameter of the distribution, θ, is the expected value of the loss function

$$R(\theta, \hat{\theta}) = \mathbb{E}_\theta L(\theta, \hat{\theta}) = \int L(\theta, \hat{\theta})\, dP_\theta.$$

Chapter 8. Making Decisions

where dP_θ is a probability measure parametrized by θ.

- For a scalar parameter θ and a quadratic loss function,

$$L(\theta, \hat{\theta}) = (\theta - \hat{\theta})^2$$

the _____ function becomes the mean squared error of the estimate,

$$R(\theta, \hat{\theta}) = E_\theta (\theta - \hat{\theta})^2$$

- In density estimation, the unknown parameter is probability density itself. The loss function is typically chosen to be a norm in an appropriate function space. For example, for L^2 norm,

$$L(f, \hat{f}) = \|f - \hat{f}\|_2^2$$

the _____ function becomes the mean integrated squared error

$$R(f, \hat{f}) = E\|f - \hat{f}\|^2$$

a. Financial modeling
b. Risk aversion
c. Risk
d. Linear model

19. A _____ is a decision support tool that uses a tree-like graph or model of decisions and their possible consequences, including chance event outcomes, resource costs, and utility. _____s are commonly used in operations research, specifically in decision analysis, to help identify a strategy most likely to reach a goal. Another use of _____s is as a descriptive means for calculating conditional probabilities.
   a. 28-hour day
   b. 33 Strategies of War
   c. Decision tree
   d. 1990 Clean Air Act

20. _____ is the largest book retailer in the United States, operating mainly through its Barnes ' Noble Booksellers chain of bookstores headquartered in lower Fifth Avenue in Manhattan.

The company operates the chain of small 'B.

   a. 1990 Clean Air Act
   b. 33 Strategies of War
   c. Barnes ' Noble, Inc.
   d. 28-hour day

21. _____ is the process of recruiting individuals to fill executive positions in organizations. _____ may be performed by an organization's board of directors, by executives in the organization, or by an outside _____ organization.

The _____ profession has two distinct fields, retained _____ and contingency search.

Chapter 8. Making Decisions

a. Executive Search
c. Employment agency
b. Internet recruiting
d. Employee referral

22. Appraisal is the third and last stage in using formal decision methods. The objective of the appraisal stage is for the decision maker to develop insight into the decision and determine a clear course of action. Much of the insight developed in this stage results from exploring the implications of the formal _____ developed during the formulation stage (i.e., from mining the model.)
   a. Decision Matrix
   c. Nominal group technique
   b. Kepner-Tregoe
   d. Decision model

23. _____ is a form of communication that typically attempts to persuade potential customers to purchase or to consume more of a particular brand of product or service. 'While now central to the contemporary global economy and the reproduction of global production networks, it is only quite recently that _____ has been more than a marginal influence on patterns of sales and production. The formation of modern _____ was intimately bound up with the emergence of new forms of monopoly capitalism around the end of the 19th and beginning of the 20th century as one element in corporate strategies to create, organize and where possible control markets, especially for mass produced consumer goods.
   a. AAAI
   c. A Stake in the Outcome
   b. A4e
   d. Advertising

24. While the full name of the Swiss verein is Deloitte Touche Tohmatsu, in 1989 it initially branded itself _____ and then simply Deloitte. In 2003 the rebranding campaign was commissioned by Bill Parrett, the then CEO of DTT, and led by Jerry Leamon, the global Clients and Markets leader.

Deloitte member firms offer services in the following functions, with country-specific variations on their legal implementation (i.e. all operating within a single company or through separate legal entities operating as subsidiaries of an umbrella legal entity for the country.)

   a. Deloitte ' Touche
   c. 33 Strategies of War
   b. 28-hour day
   d. 1990 Clean Air Act

25. _____ is a group creativity technique designed to generate a large number of ideas for the solution of a problem. The method was first popularized in the late 1930s by Alex Faickney Osborn in a book called Applied Imagination. Osborn proposed that groups could double their creative output with _____.
   a. Adam Smith
   c. Affiliation
   b. Abraham Harold Maslow
   d. Brainstorming

26. _____ is decision making in groups consisting of multiple members/entities. The challenge of group decision is deciding what action a group should take. There are various systems designed to solve this problem.
   a. Control of Substances Hazardous to Health Regulations 2002
   c. Collaborative Planning, Forecasting and Replenishment
   b. Groups decision making
   d. Genbutsu

27. A _____ is directly responsible for managing the day-to-day operations (and profitability) of a company.

Chapter 8. Making Decisions

Chief Executive Officer (CEO)
- As the top manager, the CEO is typically responsible for the entire operations of the corporation and reports directly to the chairman and board of directors. It is the CEO's responsibility to implement board decisions and initiatives and to maintain the smooth operation of the firm, with the assistance of senior management.

 a. Vorstand
 b. Getting Things Done
 c. Field service management
 d. Management Team

28. The _____ is a decision making method for use among groups of many sizes, who want to make their decision quickly, as by a vote, but want everyone's opinions taken into account (as opposed to traditional voting, where only the largest group is considered) . The method of tallying is the difference. First, every member of the group gives their view of the solution, with a short explanation.
 a. Belief decision matrix
 b. Decision model
 c. Hierarchical Decision Process
 d. Nominal group technique

29. _____ refers to techniques, processes and tools for organizing and coordinating a group of individuals working towards a common goal--i.e. a team.

Several well-known approaches to _____ have come out of academic work. Examples include the Belbin Team Inventory by Meredith Belbin, a method to identify the different types of personalities within teams, and Ken Blanchard's description of 'High Performing Teams'.

 a. 28-hour day
 b. 33 Strategies of War
 c. 1990 Clean Air Act
 d. Team management

30. The _____ is a systematic, interactive forecasting method which relies on a panel of independent experts. The carefully selected experts answer questionnaires in two or more rounds. After each round, a facilitator provides an anonymous summary of the experts' forecasts from the previous round as well as the reasons they provided for their judgments.
 a. Learning organization
 b. Hoshin Kanri
 c. Delphi method
 d. Quality function deployment

31. The 'business case for _____', theorizes that in a global marketplace, a company that employs a diverse workforce (both men and women, people of many generations, people from ethnically and racially diverse backgrounds etc.) is better able to understand the demographics of the marketplace it serves and is thus better equipped to thrive in that marketplace than a company that has a more limited range of employee demographics.

An additional corollary suggests that a company that supports the _____ of its workforce can also improve employee satisfaction, productivity and retention.

 a. Diversity
 b. Trademark
 c. Virtual team
 d. Kanban

Chapter 8. Making Decisions

32. _____ is a type of thought exhibited by group members who try to minimize conflict and reach consensus without critically testing, analyzing, and evaluating ideas. Individual creativity, uniqueness, and independent thinking are lost in the pursuit of group cohesiveness, as are the advantages of reasonable balance in choice and thought that might normally be obtained by making decisions as a group. During _____, members of the group avoid promoting viewpoints outside the comfort zone of consensus thinking.
    a. Diffusion of responsibility
    b. Psychological statistics
    c. Self-report inventory
    d. Groupthink

33. _____ is an advertisement in which a particular product specifically mentions a competitor by name for the express purpose of showing why the competitor is inferior to the product naming it.

This should not be confused with parody advertisements, where a fictional product is being advertised for the purpose of poking fun at the particular advertisement, nor should it be confused with the use of a coined brand name for the purpose of comparing the product without actually naming an actual competitor. ('Wikipedia tastes better and is less filling than the Encyclopedia Galactica.')

In the 1980s, during what has been referred to as the cola wars, soft-drink manufacturer Pepsi ran a series of advertisements where people, caught on hidden camera, in a blind taste test, chose Pepsi over rival Coca-Cola.

    a. 1990 Clean Air Act
    b. 33 Strategies of War
    c. Comparative advertising
    d. 28-hour day

34. _____ of the learning curve effect and the closely related experience curve effect express the relationship between equations for experience and efficiency or between efficiency gains and investment in the effort. The experience of 'learning curves' was first observed by the 19th Century German psychologist Hermann Ebbinghaus according to the difficulty of memorizing varying numbers of verbal stimuli, and subsequent learning about the complex processes of learning are discussed in the

.

The rule used for representing the learning curve effect states that the more times a task has been performed, the less time will be required on each subsequent iteration.

    a. Spatial Decision Support Systems
    b. Point biserial correlation coefficient
    c. Distribution
    d. Models

35. _____ is an inventory strategy that strives to improve the return on investment of a business by reducing in-process inventory and its associated carrying costs. To meet _____ objectives, the process relies on signals between different points in the process. This means the process is often driven by a series of signals, or Kanban , which tell production when to make the next part. Kanban are usually 'tickets' but can be simple visual signals, such as the presence or absence of a part on a shelf. Implemented correctly, _____ can dramatically improve a manufacturing organization's return on investment, quality, and efficiency.
    a. 28-hour day
    b. 1990 Clean Air Act
    c. Just-in-time
    d. 33 Strategies of War

Chapter 9. Organizing Principles

1. _____ is a Japanese philosophy that focuses on continuous improvement throughout all aspects of life. When applied to the workplace, _____ activities continually improve all functions of a business, from manufacturing to management and from the CEO to the assembly line workers. By improving standardized activities and processes, _____ aims to eliminate waste .

   a. Psychological pricing
   b. Sensitivity analysis
   c. Cross-docking
   d. Kaizen

2. _____ is an advertisement in which a particular product specifically mentions a competitor by name for the express purpose of showing why the competitor is inferior to the product naming it.

This should not be confused with parody advertisements, where a fictional product is being advertised for the purpose of poking fun at the particular advertisement, nor should it be confused with the use of a coined brand name for the purpose of comparing the product without actually naming an actual competitor. ('Wikipedia tastes better and is less filling than the Encyclopedia Galactica.')

In the 1980s, during what has been referred to as the cola wars, soft-drink manufacturer Pepsi ran a series of advertisements where people, caught on hidden camera, in a blind taste test, chose Pepsi over rival Coca-Cola.

   a. 33 Strategies of War
   b. 28-hour day
   c. 1990 Clean Air Act
   d. Comparative advertising

3. _____ is something that a firm can do well and that meets the following three conditions:

Competencies are things that companys execute well across several business units or product sectors.

Firms usually have few competencies, but these are usually less liable to change rapidly.

1. It provides consumer benefits
2. It is not easy for competitors to imitate
3. It can be leveraged widely to many products and markets.

A _____ can take various forms, including technical/subject matter know-how, a reliable process and/or close relationships with customers and suppliers (Mascarenhas et al. 1998.)

   a. Dominant Design
   b. NAIRU
   c. Learning-by-doing
   d. Core competency

4. _____ is subcontracting a process, such as product design or manufacturing, to a third-party company. The decision to outsource is often made in the interest of lowering cost or making better use of time and energy costs, redirecting or conserving energy directed at the competencies of a particular business, or to make more efficient use of land, labor, capital, (information) technology and resources. _____ became part of the business lexicon during the 1980s.

   a. Operant conditioning
   b. Opinion leadership
   c. Unemployment insurance
   d. Outsourcing

Chapter 9. Organizing Principles

5. _____ is a fixed set of rules of intra-organization procedures and structures. As such, it is usually set out in writing, with a language of rules that ostensibly leave little discretion for interpretation. In some societies and in some organization, such rules may be strictly followed; in others, they may be little more than an empty formalism.
   a. 1990 Clean Air Act
   b. 28-hour day
   c. Formal organization
   d. 33 Strategies of War

6. In a military context, the _____ is the line of authority and responsibility along which orders are passed within a military unit and between different units. The term is also used in a civilian management context describing comparable hierarchical structures of authority.
   a. 1990 Clean Air Act
   b. Chain of command
   c. 28-hour day
   d. French leave

7. _____ is an organization's process of defining its strategy and making decisions on allocating its resources to pursue this strategy, including its capital and people. Various business analysis techniques can be used in _____, including SWOT analysis (Strengths, Weaknesses, Opportunities, and Threats) and PEST analysis (Political, Economic, Social, and Technological analysis) or STEER analysis involving Socio-cultural, Technological, Economic, Ecological, and Regulatory factors and EPISTEL (Environment, Political, Informatic, Social, Technological, Economic and Legal)

_____ is the formal consideration of an organization's future course. All _____ deals with at least one of three key questions:

   1. 'What do we do?'
   2. 'For whom do we do it?'
   3. 'How do we excel?'

In business _____, the third question is better phrased 'How can we beat or avoid competition?'. (Bradford and Duncan, page 1.)

   a. 1990 Clean Air Act
   b. 28-hour day
   c. 33 Strategies of War
   d. Strategic planning

8. _____ describes the situation when output from (or information about the result of) an event or phenomenon in the past will influence the same event/phenomenon in the present or future. When an event is part of a chain of cause-and-effect that forms a circuit or loop, then the event is said to 'feed back' into itself.

_____ is also a synonym for:

- _____ signal; the information about the initial event that is the basis for subsequent modification of the event.
- _____ loop; the causal path that leads from the initial generation of the _____ signal to the subsequent modification of the event.

_____ is a mechanism, process or signal that is looped back to control a system within itself. Such a loop is called a _____ loop.

Chapter 9. Organizing Principles

a. Positive feedback
b. Feedback
c. 1990 Clean Air Act
d. Feedback loop

9. A _____ is a relatively new executive level position at a corporation, company, organization typically reporting directly to the CEO or board of directors. The _____ is responsible for a brand's image, experience, and promise, and propagating it throughout all aspects of the company. The brand officer oversees marketing, advertising, design, public relations and customer service departments.
    a. Director of communications
    b. Purchasing manager
    c. Chief executive officer
    d. Chief brand officer

10. Procter is a surname, and may also refer to:

    - Bryan Waller Procter (pseud. Barry Cornwall), English poet
    - Goodwin Procter, American law firm
    - _____, consumer products multinational

    a. Strict liability
    b. Master and Servant Acts
    c. Downstream
    d. Procter ' Gamble

11. _____ is a Fortune 500, American multinational corporation headquartered in Cincinnati, Ohio, that manufactures a wide range of consumer goods. As of 2008, P'G is the 8th largest corporation in the world by market capitalization and 14th largest US company by profit.
    a. STAR
    b. Procter ' Gamble Co.
    c. Turnover
    d. Maturity of Organizations and Business Excellence - The Four-Phase Model

12. _____ refers to the process of grouping activities into departments.

    Division of labour creates specialists who need coordination. This coordination is facilitated by grouping specialists together in departments.

    a. Decent work
    b. Maximum wage
    c. Departmentalization
    d. Division of labour

13. _____ is one of the managerial functions like planning, organizing, staffing and directing. It is an important function because it helps to check the errors and to take the corrective action so that deviation from standards are minimized and stated goals of the organization are achieved in desired manner. According to modern concepts, _____ is a foreseeing action whereas earlier concept of _____ was used only when errors were detected. _____ in management means setting standards, measuring actual performance and taking corrective action.
    a. Turnover
    b. Decision tree pruning
    c. Control
    d. Schedule of reinforcement

14. An _____, or organogram(me)) is a diagram that shows the structure of an organization and the relationships and relative ranks of its parts and positions/jobs. The term is also used for similar diagrams, for example ones showing the different elements of a field of knowledge or a group of languages. The French Encyclopédie had one of the first _____s of knowledge in general.

   a. AAAI
   b. A4e
   c. A Stake in the Outcome
   d. Organizational chart

15. _____ is a term originating in military organization theory, but now used more commonly in business management, particularly human resource management. _____ refers to the number of subordinates a supervisor has.

In the hierarchical business organization of the past it was not uncommon to see average spans of 1 to 10 or even less. That is, one manager supervised ten employees on average.

   a. Senior management
   b. Mentoring
   c. Span of control
   d. CIFMS

16. The _____ is a standardized, on-scene, all-hazard incident management concept. It is a management protocol originally designed for emergency management agencies in the United States which was later federalized there. It has since been adopted by agencies in other countries.

   a. A4e
   b. AAAI
   c. Incident Command Structure
   d. A Stake in the Outcome

17. _____ is the process of recruiting individuals to fill executive positions in organizations. _____ may be performed by an organization's board of directors, by executives in the organization, or by an outside _____ organization.

The _____ profession has two distinct fields, retained _____ and contingency search.

   a. Internet recruiting
   b. Employment agency
   c. Employee referral
   d. Executive Search

18. _____ is individual power based on a high level of identification with, admiration of, or respect for the powerholder.

Nationalism, Patriotism, Celebrities and well-respected people are examples of _____ in effect.

_____ is one of the Five Bases of Social Power, as defined by Bertram Raven and his colleagues[1] in 1959.

   a. 1990 Clean Air Act
   b. Referent power
   c. 28-hour day
   d. 33 Strategies of War

19. _____ is a form of communication that typically attempts to persuade potential customers to purchase or to consume more of a particular brand of product or service. 'While now central to the contemporary global economy and the reproduction of global production networks, it is only quite recently that _____ has been more than a marginal influence on patterns of sales and production. The formation of modern _____ was intimately bound up with the emergence of new forms of monopoly capitalism around the end of the 19th and beginning of the 20th century as one element in corporate strategies to create, organize and where possible control markets, especially for mass produced consumer goods.

Chapter 9. Organizing Principles

    a. A Stake in the Outcome   b. A4e
    c. Advertising   d. AAAI

20. _____ is a concept in ethics with several meanings. It is often used synonymously with such concepts as responsibility, answerability, enforcement, blameworthiness, liability and other terms associated with the expectation of account-giving. As an aspect of governance, it has been central to discussions related to problems in both the public and private (corporation) worlds.
    a. Usury   b. A4e
    c. A Stake in the Outcome   d. Accountability

21. _____ refers to increasing the spiritual, political, social or economic strength of individuals and communities. It often involves the empowered developing confidence in their own capacities.

The term Human _____ covers a vast landscape of meanings, interpretations, definitions and disciplines ranging from psychology and philosophy to the highly commercialized Self-Help industry and Motivational sciences.

    a. AAAI   b. A4e
    c. A Stake in the Outcome   d. Empowerment

22. _____ is the process by which the activities of an organisation, particularly those regarding decision-making, become concentrated within a particular location and/or group.
    a. Corner office   b. Chief operating officer
    c. Product innovation   d. Centralization

23. _____ is the process of dispersing decision-making governance closer to the people or citizen. It includes the dispersal of administration or governance in sectors or areas like engineering, management science, political science, political economy, sociology and economics. _____ is also possible in the dispersal of population and employment.
    a. Formula for Change   b. Frenemy
    c. Business plan   d. Decentralization

24. A _____ is directly responsible for managing the day-to-day operations (and profitability) of a company.

Chief Executive Officer (CEO)
    - As the top manager, the CEO is typically responsible for the entire operations of the corporation and reports directly to the chairman and board of directors. It is the CEO's responsibility to implement board decisions and initiatives and to maintain the smooth operation of the firm, with the assistance of senior management.

    a. Field service management   b. Getting Things Done
    c. Management Team   d. Vorstand

25. _____ refers to techniques, processes and tools for organizing and coordinating a group of individuals working towards a common goal--i.e. a team.

Several well-known approaches to _____ have come out of academic work. Examples include the Belbin Team Inventory by Meredith Belbin, a method to identify the different types of personalities within teams, and Ken Blanchard's description of 'High Performing Teams'.

    a. 1990 Clean Air Act
    b. 33 Strategies of War
    c. Team management
    d. 28-hour day

26. The _____ was a period in the late 18th and early 19th centuries when major changes in agriculture, manufacturing, mining, and transportation had a profound effect on the socioeconomic and cultural conditions in Britain. The changes subsequently spread throughout Europe, North America, and eventually the world. The onset of the _____ marked a major turning point in human society; almost every aspect of daily life was eventually influenced in some way.

    a. Abraham Harold Maslow
    b. Industrial Revolution
    c. Affiliation
    d. Adam Smith

27. The _____ is the interlocking social structure that governs how people work together in practice. It is the aggregate of behaviors, interactions, norms, personal and professional connections through which work gets done and relationships are built among people who share a common organizational affiliation or cluster of affiliations. It consists of a dynamic set of personal relationships, social networks, communities of common interest, and emotional sources of motivation. The _____ evolves organically and spontaneously in response to changes in the work environment, the flux of people through its porous boundaries, and the complex social dynamics of its members.

    a. Open shop
    b. Informal organization
    c. Union shop
    d. Organizational effectiveness

28. In economics, business, retail, and accounting, a _____ is the value of money that has been used up to produce something, and hence is not available for use anymore. In economics, a _____ is an alternative that is given up as a result of a decision. In business, the _____ may be one of acquisition, in which case the amount of money expended to acquire it is counted as _____.

    a. Cost overrun
    b. Cost allocation
    c. Cost
    d. Fixed costs

29. _____ is the provision of service to customers before, during and after a purchase.

According to Turban et al. (2002), '_____ is a series of activities designed to enhance the level of customer satisfaction - that is, the feeling that a product or service has met the customer expectation.'

Its importance varies by product, industry and customer; defective or broken merchandise can be exchanged, often only with a receipt and within a specified time frame.

    a. Customer Service
    b. 28-hour day
    c. Service rate
    d. 1990 Clean Air Act

30. _____ is the state or fact of exclusive rights and control over property, which may be an object, land/real estate or intellectual property. An _____ right is also referred to as title. The concept of _____ has existed for thousands of years and in all cultures.

Chapter 9. Organizing Principles

a. A4e
b. Ownership
c. Emanation of the state
d. A Stake in the Outcome

31. In economics, and cost accounting, _____ describes the total economic cost of production and is made up of variable costs, which vary according to the quantity of a good produced and include inputs such as labor and raw materials, plus fixed costs, which are independent of the quantity of a good produced and include inputs (capital) that cannot be varied in the short term, such as buildings and machinery. _____ in economics includes the total opportunity cost of each factor of production in addition to fixed and variable costs.

The rate at which _____ changes as the amount produced changes is called marginal cost.

a. 28-hour day
b. 33 Strategies of War
c. 1990 Clean Air Act
d. Total Cost

32. _____ is a financial estimate designed to help consumers and enterprise managers assess direct and indirect costs It is a form of full cost accounting.

a. 33 Strategies of War
b. 28-hour day
c. 1990 Clean Air Act
d. Total Cost of Ownership

33. _____ is the life cycle of an organization from birth level to the termination.

There are five level/stages in any organization.

1. Birth
2. Growth
3. Maturity
4. Decline
5. Death

According to Richard L. Daft there are four stages in an _____.

The four stages are:

1. Entrepreneurial stage -> Crisis: Need for leadership
2. Collectivity stage -> Crisis: Need for delegation
3. Formalization stage -> Crisis: Too much red tape
4. Elaboration stage -> Crisis: Need for revitalization

(Richard L. Daft, Understanding the Theory and Design of Organizations, first edition 2007, ISBN 0-324-42271-7)

a. A4e
b. A Stake in the Outcome
c. AAAI
d. Organizational life cycle

Chapter 9. Organizing Principles

34. _____ is 'interfirm coordination that is characterized by organic or informal social systems, in contrast to bureaucratic structures within firms and formal contractual relationships between them.(Gerlach, 1992:64; Nohria, 1992)' A useful survey of network organization theory appears in Van Alstyne (1997).

The concepts of privatization, public private partnership, and contracting are defined in this context.

As a concept, _____ explains increased efficiency and reduced agency problems for organizations existing in highly turbulent environments . Due to the rapid pace of modern society and competitive pressures from globalization, _____ has gained prominence and development among sociological theorists. As a concept, _____ explains increased efficiency and reduced agency problems for organizations existing in highly turbulent environments.

    a. 33 Strategies of War
    c. 1990 Clean Air Act
    b. 28-hour day
    d. Network governance

35. In probability theory, a probability distribution is called _____ if its cumulative distribution function is _____. This is equivalent to saying that for random variables X with the distribution in question, Pr[X = a] = 0 for all real numbers a, i.e.: the probability that X attains the value a is zero, for any number a. If the distribution of X is _____ then X is called a _____ random variable.

    a. Connectionist expert systems
    c. Decision tree pruning
    b. Pay Band
    d. Continuous

36. A _____ system is a manufacturing system in which there is some amount of flexibility that allows the system to react in the case of changes, whether predicted or unpredicted. This flexibility is generally considered to fall into two categories, which both contain numerous subcategories.

The first category, machine flexibility, covers the system's ability to be changed to produce new product types, and ability to change the order of operations executed on a part. The second category is called routing flexibility, which consists of the ability to use multiple machines to perform the same operation on a part, as well as the system's ability to absorb large-scale changes, such as in volume, capacity, or capability.

    a. Manufacturing resource planning
    c. Homeworkers
    b. Jidoka
    d. Flexible manufacturing

37. Maslow's _____ is a theory in psychology, proposed by Abraham Maslow in his 1943 paper A Theory of Human Motivation, which he subsequently extended to include his observations of humans' innate curiosity.

Maslow's _____ is predetermined in order of importance. It is often depicted as a pyramid consisting of five levels: the lowest level is associated with physiological needs, while the uppermost level is associated with self-actualization needs, particularly those related to identity and purpose. Deficiency needs must be met first. Once these are met, seeking to satisfy growth needs drives personal growth. The higher needs in this hierarchy only come into focus when the lower needs in the pyramid are met.

Chapter 9. Organizing Principles

a. 33 Strategies of War
b. 28-hour day
c. Hierarchy of needs
d. 1990 Clean Air Act

38. _____ is the production of large amounts of standardized products, including and especially on assembly lines. The concepts of _____ are applied to various kinds of products, from fluids and particulates handled in bulk to discrete solid parts to assemblies of such parts

_____ of assemblies typically uses electric-motor-powered moving tracks or conveyor belts to move partially complete products to workers, who perform simple repetitive tasks.

a. Mass production
b. 33 Strategies of War
c. 1990 Clean Air Act
d. 28-hour day

39. An _____ is a mostly hierarchical concept of subordination of entities that collaborate and contribute to serve one common aim.

Organizations are a variant of clustered entities. The structure of an organization is usually set up in many a styles, dependent on their objectives and ambience.

a. Informal organization
b. Open shop
c. Organizational development
d. Organizational structure

40. Quality management can be considered to have three main components: quality control, quality assurance and _____. Quality management is focused not only on product quality, but also the means to achieve it. Quality management therefore uses quality assurance and control of processes as well as products to achieve more consistent quality.

a. Quality management
b. Quality improvement
c. 28-hour day
d. 1990 Clean Air Act

41. In finance, an _____ is a contract between a buyer and a seller that gives the buyer the right--but not the obligation--to buy or to sell a particular asset (the underlying asset) at a later day at an agreed price. In return for granting the _____, the seller collects a payment (the premium) from the buyer. A call _____ gives the buyer the right to buy the underlying asset; a put _____ gives the buyer of the _____ the right to sell the underlying asset.

a. AAAI
b. A Stake in the Outcome
c. A4e
d. Option

Chapter 10. Organizational Design

1. _____ is understood as a business unit within the overall corporate identity which is distinguishable from other business because it serves a defined external market where management can conduct strategic planning in relation to products and markets. When companies become really large, they are best thought of as being composed of a number of businesses (or _____s.)

In the broader domain of strategic management, the phrase '_____' came into use in the 1960s, largely as a result of General Electric's many units.

   a. Strategic drift
   b. Strategic group
   c. Switching cost
   d. Strategic business unit

2. _____, in microeconomics, are the cost advantages that a business obtains due to expansion. They are factors that cause a producer's average cost per unit to fall as scale is increased. _____ is a long run concept and refers to reductions in unit cost as the size of a facility, or scale, increases.

   a. A Stake in the Outcome
   b. Economies of scope
   c. A4e
   d. Economies of scale

3. _____ refers to the long-term management of intractable conflicts. It is the label for the variety of ways by which people handle grievances--standing up for what they consider to be right and against what they consider to be wrong. Those ways include such diverse phenomena as gossip, ridicule, lynching, terrorism, warfare, feuding, genocide, law, mediation, and avoidance.

   a. 28-hour day
   b. 33 Strategies of War
   c. Conflict management
   d. 1990 Clean Air Act

4. Organizational culture is not the same as _____. It is wider and deeper concepts, something that an organization 'is' rather than what it 'has' (according to Buchanan and Huczynski.)

_____ is the total sum of the values, customs, traditions and meanings that make a company unique.

   a. Path-goal theory
   b. Job analysis
   c. Work design
   d. Corporate Culture

5. _____ is the process of recruiting individuals to fill executive positions in organizations. _____ may be performed by an organization's board of directors, by executives in the organization, or by an outside _____ organization.

The _____ profession has two distinct fields, retained _____ and contingency search.

   a. Employee referral
   b. Executive Search
   c. Internet recruiting
   d. Employment agency

6. _____, widely known as F. W. Taylor, was an American mechanical engineer who sought to improve industrial efficiency. He is regarded as the father of scientific management, and was one of the first management consultants.

Taylor was one of the intellectual leaders of the Efficiency Movement and his ideas, broadly conceived, were highly influential in the Progressive Era.

Chapter 10. Organizational Design

    a. Geoffrey Colvin
    b. Douglas N. Daft
    c. Frederick Winslow Taylor
    d. Jonah Jacob Goldberg

7. An _____ is a private network that uses Internet protocols, network connectivity, and possibly the public telecommunication system to securely share part of an organization's information or operations with suppliers, vendors, partners, customers or other businesses. An _____ can be viewed as part of a company's intranet that is extended to users outside the company (e.g.: normally over the Internet.) It has also been described as a 'state of mind' in which the Internet is perceived as a way to do business with a preapproved set of other companies business-to-business (B2B), in isolation from all other Internet users.

    a. A4e
    b. AAAI
    c. A Stake in the Outcome
    d. Extranet

8. An _____ is a private computer network that uses Internet technologies to securely share any part of an organization's information or operational systems with its employees. Sometimes the term refers only to the organization's internal website, but often it is a more extensive part of the organization's computer infrastructure and private websites are an important component and focal point of internal communication and collaboration.

An _____ is built from the same concepts and technologies used for the Internet, such as client-server computing and the Internet Protocol Suite (TCP/IP.)

    a. AAAI
    b. Intranet
    c. A Stake in the Outcome
    d. A4e

9. _____ is the provision of service to customers before, during and after a purchase.

According to Turban et al. (2002), '_____ is a series of activities designed to enhance the level of customer satisfaction - that is, the feeling that a product or service has met the customer expectation.'

Its importance varies by product, industry and customer; defective or broken merchandise can be exchanged, often only with a receipt and within a specified time frame.

    a. Service rate
    b. 28-hour day
    c. Customer Service
    d. 1990 Clean Air Act

10. Procter is a surname, and may also refer to:

- Bryan Waller Procter (pseud. Barry Cornwall), English poet
- Goodwin Procter, American law firm
- _____, consumer products multinational

    a. Strict liability
    b. Downstream
    c. Master and Servant Acts
    d. Procter ' Gamble

Chapter 10. Organizational Design

11. _____ is a Fortune 500, American multinational corporation headquartered in Cincinnati, Ohio, that manufactures a wide range of consumer goods. As of 2008, P'G is the 8th largest corporation in the world by market capitalization and 14th largest US company by profit.

   a. Procter ' Gamble Co.
   b. STAR
   c. Maturity of Organizations and Business Excellence - The Four-Phase Model
   d. Turnover

12. _____ is an advertisement in which a particular product specifically mentions a competitor by name for the express purpose of showing why the competitor is inferior to the product naming it.

This should not be confused with parody advertisements, where a fictional product is being advertised for the purpose of poking fun at the particular advertisement, nor should it be confused with the use of a coined brand name for the purpose of comparing the product without actually naming an actual competitor. ('Wikipedia tastes better and is less filling than the Encyclopedia Galactica.')

In the 1980s, during what has been referred to as the cola wars, soft-drink manufacturer Pepsi ran a series of advertisements where people, caught on hidden camera, in a blind taste test, chose Pepsi over rival Coca-Cola.

   a. Comparative advertising
   b. 1990 Clean Air Act
   c. 33 Strategies of War
   d. 28-hour day

13. _____ is the life cycle of an organization from birth level to the termination.

There are five level/stages in any organization.

1. Birth
2. Growth
3. Maturity
4. Decline
5. Death

According to Richard L. Daft there are four stages in an _____.

The four stages are:

1. Entrepreneurial stage -> Crisis: Need for leadership
2. Collectivity stage -> Crisis: Need for delegation
3. Formalization stage -> Crisis: Too much red tape
4. Elaboration stage -> Crisis: Need for revitalization

(Richard L. Daft, Understanding the Theory and Design of Organizations, first edition 2007, ISBN 0-324-42271-7)

a. Organizational life cycle
b. AAAI
c. A Stake in the Outcome
d. A4e

14. The _____ is a self-assessed personality questionnaire designed to help people better understand themselves and others. It was first introduced in the book Please Understand Me. The _____ is closely associated with the Myers-Briggs Type Indicator (MBTI); however, there are significant practical and theoretical differences between the two personality questionnaires and their associated different descriptions.

a. 33 Strategies of War
b. 1990 Clean Air Act
c. 28-hour day
d. Keirsey Temperament Sorter

15. _____ is something that a firm can do well and that meets the following three conditions:

Competencies are things that companys execute well across several business units or product sectors.

Firms usually have few competencies, but these are usually less liable to change rapidly.

1. It provides consumer benefits
2. It is not easy for competitors to imitate
3. It can be leveraged widely to many products and markets.

A _____ can take various forms, including technical/subject matter know-how, a reliable process and/or close relationships with customers and suppliers (Mascarenhas et al. 1998.)

a. NAIRU
b. Dominant Design
c. Learning-by-doing
d. Core competency

Chapter 11. Organizational Structure and Change

1. _____ is an American writer on business management practices, best-known for, In Search of Excellence (co-authored with Robert H. Waterman, Jr.)

Peters was born in Baltimore, Maryland. He went to Severn School for High School and attended Cornell University, receiving a bachelor's degree in civil engineering in 1965, and a master's degree in 1966.

   a. Adam Smith
   c. Affiliation
   b. Abraham Harold Maslow
   d. Thomas J. Peters

2. Procter is a surname, and may also refer to:

   - Bryan Waller Procter (pseud. Barry Cornwall), English poet
   - Goodwin Procter, American law firm
   - _____, consumer products multinational

   a. Downstream
   c. Master and Servant Acts
   b. Strict liability
   d. Procter ' Gamble

3. _____ is a Fortune 500, American multinational corporation headquartered in Cincinnati, Ohio, that manufactures a wide range of consumer goods. As of 2008, P'G is the 8th largest corporation in the world by market capitalization and 14th largest US company by profit.

   a. Turnover
   c. STAR
   b. Maturity of Organizations and Business Excellence - The Four-Phase Model
   d. Procter ' Gamble Co.

4. In economics, the _____ is the term economists use to describe the self-regulating nature of the marketplace. The _____ is a metaphor coined by the economist Adam Smith in The Wealth of Nations.

Adam Smith mentions the metaphor in Book IV of The Wealth of Nations, arguing that people in any society will certainly employ their capital in foreign trading only if the profits available by that method far exceed those available locally, and that in such a case it is better for society as a whole if they so did.

   a. AAAI
   c. A4e
   b. A Stake in the Outcome
   d. Invisible hand

5. A _____ is a brief written statement of the purpose of a company or organization. Ideally, a _____ guides the actions of the organization, spells out its overall goal, provides a sense of direction, and guides decision making for all levels of management.

_____s often contain the following:

   - Purpose and aim of the organization
   - The organization's primary stakeholders: clients, stockholders, etc.
   - Responsibilities of the organization toward these stakeholders
   - Products and services offered

Chapter 11. Organizational Structure and Change

In developing a _____:

- Encourage as much input as feasible from employees, volunteers, and other stakeholders
- Publicize it broadly

The _____ can be used to resolve differences between business stakeholders. Stakeholders include: employees including managers and executives, stockholders, board of directors, customers, suppliers, distributors, creditors, governments (local, state, federal, etc.), unions, competitors, NGO's, and the general public.

a. 28-hour day
b. 1990 Clean Air Act
c. Mission statement
d. 33 Strategies of War

6. _____ is an idea in the field of Organizational studies and management which describes the psychology, attitudes, experiences, beliefs and Values (personal and cultural values) of an organization. It has been defined as 'the specific collection of values and norms that are shared by people and groups in an organization and that control the way they interact with each other and with stakeholders outside the organization.'

This definition continues to explain organizational values also known as 'beliefs and ideas about what kinds of goals members of an organization should pursue and ideas about the appropriate kinds or standards of behavior organizational members should use to achieve these goals. From organizational values develop organizational norms, guidelines or expectations that prescribe appropriate kinds of behavior by employees in particular situations and control the behavior of organizational members towards one another.'

_____ is not the same as corporate culture.

a. Organizational effectiveness
b. Organizational development
c. Organizational culture
d. Union shop

7. While the full name of the Swiss verein is Deloitte Touche Tohmatsu, in 1989 it initially branded itself _____ and then simply Deloitte. In 2003 the rebranding campaign was commissioned by Bill Parrett, the then CEO of DTT, and led by Jerry Leamon, the global Clients and Markets leader.

Deloitte member firms offer services in the following functions, with country-specific variations on their legal implementation (i.e. all operating within a single company or through separate legal entities operating as subsidiaries of an umbrella legal entity for the country.)

a. 28-hour day
b. 33 Strategies of War
c. 1990 Clean Air Act
d. Deloitte ' Touche

8. The 'business case for _____', theorizes that in a global marketplace, a company that employs a diverse workforce (both men and women, people of many generations, people from ethnically and racially diverse backgrounds etc.) is better able to understand the demographics of the marketplace it serves and is thus better equipped to thrive in that marketplace than a company that has a more limited range of employee demographics.

An additional corollary suggests that a company that supports the _____ of its workforce can also improve employee satisfaction, productivity and retention.

   a. Virtual team
   c. Trademark
   b. Diversity
   d. Kanban

9. The _____ was a period in the late 18th and early 19th centuries when major changes in agriculture, manufacturing, mining, and transportation had a profound effect on the socioeconomic and cultural conditions in Britain. The changes subsequently spread throughout Europe, North America, and eventually the world. The onset of the _____ marked a major turning point in human society; almost every aspect of daily life was eventually influenced in some way.

   a. Affiliation
   c. Industrial Revolution
   b. Adam Smith
   d. Abraham Harold Maslow

10. The _____ is the interlocking social structure that governs how people work together in practice. It is the aggregate of behaviors, interactions, norms, personal and professional connections through which work gets done and relationships are built among people who share a common organizational affiliation or cluster of affiliations. It consists of a dynamic set of personal relationships, social networks, communities of common interest, and emotional sources of motivation. The _____ evolves organically and spontaneously in response to changes in the work environment, the flux of people through its porous boundaries, and the complex social dynamics of its members.

   a. Union shop
   c. Open shop
   b. Organizational effectiveness
   d. Informal organization

11. _____ is the process of recruiting individuals to fill executive positions in organizations. _____ may be performed by an organization's board of directors, by executives in the organization, or by an outside _____ organization.

The _____ profession has two distinct fields, retained _____ and contingency search.

   a. Employment agency
   c. Internet recruiting
   b. Employee referral
   d. Executive Search

12. In sociology, anthropology and cultural studies, a _____ is a group of people with a culture (whether distinct or hidden) which differentiates them from the larger culture to which they belong. If a particular _____ is characterized by a systematic opposition to the dominant culture, it may be described as a counterculture.

As early as 1950, David Riesman distinguished between a majority, 'which passively accepted commercially provided styles and meanings, and a '_____' which actively sought a minority style ...

   a. 1990 Clean Air Act
   c. Subculture
   b. 28-hour day
   d. 33 Strategies of War

13. _____ is a broad label that refers to any individuals or households that use goods and services generated within the economy. The concept of a _____ is used in different contexts, so that the usage and significance of the term may vary.

Typically when business people and economists talk of _____s they are talking about person as _____, an aggregated commodity item with little individuality other than that expressed in the buy/not-buy decision.

a. 1990 Clean Air Act
b. 33 Strategies of War
c. Consumer
d. 28-hour day

14. The _____ is given by the United States National Institute of Standards and Technology. Through the actions of the National Productivity Advisory Committee chaired by Jack Grayson, it was established by the Malcolm Baldrige National Quality Improvement Act of 1987 - Public Law 100-107 and named for Malcolm Baldrige, who served as United States Secretary of Commerce during the Reagan administration from 1981 until his 1987 death in a rodeo accident. APQC, , organized the first White House Conference on Productivity, spearheading the creation and design of the _____ in 1987, and jointly administering the award for its first three years.

a. Scenario planning
b. Business Network Transformation
c. Time and attendance
d. Malcolm Baldrige National Quality Award

15. _____ is a strategic planning method used to evaluate the Strengths, Weaknesses, Opportunities, and Threats involved in a project or in a business venture. It involves specifying the objective of the business venture or project and identifying the internal and external factors that are favorable and unfavorable to achieving that objective. The technique is credited to Albert Humphrey, who led a convention at Stanford University in the 1960s and 1970s using data from Fortune 500 companies.

a. Market share
b. Marketing
c. Corporate image
d. SWOT analysis

16. An _____ details guidelines, expectations and procedures of a business or company to its employees.

_____s are given to employees on one of the first days of his/her job, in order to acquaint them with their new company and its policies.

Chapter 11. Organizational Structure and Change

While it often varies from business to business, specific areas that an _____ may address include:

- A welcome statement, which may also briefly describe the company's history, reasons for its success and how the employee can contribute to future successes. It may also include a mission statement, or a statement about a business' goals and objectives.
- Orientation procedures. This usually involves providing a human resources manager or other designated employee completed income tax withholding forms, providing proof of identity and eligibility for employment (in accordance with the Immigration Reform and Control Act of 1986), proof of a completed drug test (by a designated medical center) and other required forms.
- Definitions of full- and part-time employment, and benefits each classification receives. In addition, this area also describes timekeeping procedures (such as defining a 'work week'.) This area may also include information about daily breaks (for lunch and rest.)
- Information about employee pay and benefits (such as vacation and insurance.) Usually, new employees are awarded some benefits, plus additional rewards (such as enrollment in a 401K retirement account program, additional vacation and pay raises) after having worked for a company for a certain period of time. These are spelled out in this section.
- Expectations about conduct and discipline policies. These sections include conduct policies for such areas as sexual harassment, alcohol and drug use, and attendance; plus, grounds for dismissal (i.e., getting fired) and due process. This area may also include information about filing grievances with supervisors and/or co-workers, and communicating work-related issues with supervisors and/or company managers.
- Guidelines for employee performance reviews (such as how and when they are conducted.)
- Policies for promotion or demotion to a certain position.
- Rules concerning mail; use of the telephone, company equipment, Internet and e-mail; and employee use of motor vehicles for job assignments.
- Procedures on handling on-the-job accidents, such as those that result in injury.
- How an employee may voluntarily terminate his job (through retirement or resignation), and exit interviews.
- A requirement that employees keep certain business information confidential. This area usually includes information about releasing employee records and information, as well as who may retrieve and inspect the information.

If the employer is covered by the Family and Medical Leave Act of 1993 - generally 50 or more employees - a handbook must have information about FMLA.

New employees are usually required to sign a form stating they have read and understand the information, and accept the terms of the _____.

a. Underemployment
b. Employee handbook
c. Employment
d. Informational interview

17. _____ is a term used in general business practice to describe methodologies, systems, and practices designed to generate new potential business clientele, generally operated through a variety of marketing techniques. _____ facilitates a business's connection between its outgoing consumer advertising and the responses to that advertising. These processes are designed for business-to-business and direct-to-consumer strategies.

Chapter 11. Organizational Structure and Change

a. 1990 Clean Air Act
b. Lead generation
c. Request for Proposal
d. Lead Management

18. _____ refers to both the industry of, and the practice of, helping organizations improve their performance, primarily through the analysis of existing business problems and development of plans for improvement.

Organizations hire the services of management consultants for a number of reasons, including gaining external (and presumably objective) advice, access to the consultants' specialized expertise, or simply as extra temporary help during a one-time project, where the hiring of more permanent employees is not required.

Because of their exposure to and relationships with numerous organizations, consultancies are also said to be aware of industry 'best practices', although the transferability of such practices from one organization to another is the subject of debate.

a. 33 Strategies of War
b. 1990 Clean Air Act
c. 28-hour day
d. Management Consulting

19. In neuroscience, the _____ is a collection of brain structures which attempts to regulate and control behavior by inducing pleasurable effects.

A psychological reward is a process that reinforces behavior -- something that, when offered, causes a behavior to increase in intensity. Reward is an operational concept for describing the positive value an individual ascribes to an object, behavioral act or an internal physical state.

a. 1990 Clean Air Act
b. 28-hour day
c. 33 Strategies of War
d. Reward system

20. Organizational culture is not the same as _____. It is wider and deeper concepts, something that an organization 'is' rather than what it 'has' (according to Buchanan and Huczynski.)

_____ is the total sum of the values, customs, traditions and meanings that make a company unique.

a. Corporate Culture
b. Work design
c. Job analysis
d. Path-goal theory

21. _____ is an increasingly broadening term with which an organization, or other human system describes the combination of traditionally administrative personnel functions with acquisition and application of skills, knowledge and experience, Employee Relations and resource planning at various levels. The field draws upon concepts developed in Industrial/Organizational Psychology and System Theory. _____ has at least two related interpretations depending on context. The original usage derives from political economy and economics, where it was traditionally called labor, one of four factors of production although this perspective is changing as a function of new and ongoing research into more strategic approaches at national levels. This first usage is used more in terms of '_____ development', and can go beyond just organizations to the level of nations . The more traditional usage within corporations and businesses refers to the individuals within a firm or agency, and to the portion of the organization that deals with hiring, firing, training, and other personnel issues, typically referred to as `_____ management'.

Chapter 11. Organizational Structure and Change

a. Progressive discipline
b. Bradford Factor
c. Human resource management
d. Human Resources

22. In probability theory, a probability distribution is called _____ if its cumulative distribution function is _____. This is equivalent to saying that for random variables X with the distribution in question, Pr[X = a] = 0 for all real numbers a, i.e.: the probability that X attains the value a is zero, for any number a. If the distribution of X is _____ then X is called a _____ random variable.
  a. Connectionist expert systems
  b. Decision tree pruning
  c. Pay Band
  d. Continuous

23. _____ is a management process whereby delivery (customer valued) processes are constantly evaluated and improved in the light of their efficiency, effectiveness and flexibility.

Some see it as a meta process for most management systems (Business Process Management, Quality Management, Project Management). Deming saw it as part of the 'system' whereby feedback from the process and customer were evaluated against organisational goals.

  a. Sole proprietorship
  b. Continuous Improvement Process
  c. Critical Success Factor
  d. First-mover advantage

24. An _____ is a mostly hierarchical concept of subordination of entities that collaborate and contribute to serve one common aim.

Organizations are a variant of clustered entities. The structure of an organization is usually set up in many a styles, dependent on their objectives and ambience.

  a. Organizational development
  b. Open shop
  c. Informal organization
  d. Organizational structure

25. In economics, business, retail, and accounting, a _____ is the value of money that has been used up to produce something, and hence is not available for use anymore. In economics, a _____ is an alternative that is given up as a result of a decision. In business, the _____ may be one of acquisition, in which case the amount of money expended to acquire it is counted as _____.
  a. Fixed costs
  b. Cost allocation
  c. Cost overrun
  d. Cost

26. _____ is a Japanese philosophy that focuses on continuous improvement throughout all aspects of life. When applied to the workplace, _____ activities continually improve all functions of a business, from manufacturing to management and from the CEO to the assembly line workers. By improving standardized activities and processes, _____ aims to eliminate waste .
  a. Psychological pricing
  b. Sensitivity analysis
  c. Kaizen
  d. Cross-docking

27. _____ is the state or fact of exclusive rights and control over property, which may be an object, land/real estate or intellectual property. An _____ right is also referred to as title. The concept of _____ has existed for thousands of years and in all cultures.

a. A4e
b. A Stake in the Outcome
c. Emanation of the state
d. Ownership

28. In economics, and cost accounting, _____ describes the total economic cost of production and is made up of variable costs, which vary according to the quantity of a good produced and include inputs such as labor and raw materials, plus fixed costs, which are independent of the quantity of a good produced and include inputs (capital) that cannot be varied in the short term, such as buildings and machinery. _____ in economics includes the total opportunity cost of each factor of production in addition to fixed and variable costs.

The rate at which _____ changes as the amount produced changes is called marginal cost.

a. 33 Strategies of War
b. 28-hour day
c. 1990 Clean Air Act
d. Total Cost

29. _____ is a financial estimate designed to help consumers and enterprise managers assess direct and indirect costs It is a form of full cost accounting.
a. 1990 Clean Air Act
b. 28-hour day
c. 33 Strategies of War
d. Total Cost of Ownership

30. _____ is the process of comparing the cost, cycle time, productivity, or quality of a specific process or method to another that is widely considered to be an industry standard or best practice. Essentially, _____ provides a snapshot of the performance of your business and helps you understand where you are in relation to a particular standard. The result is often a business case for making changes in order to make improvements.
a. Cost leadership
b. Complementors
c. Competitive heterogeneity
d. Benchmarking

31. _____ is one of the managerial functions like planning, organizing, staffing and directing. It is an important function because it helps to check the errors and to take the corrective action so that deviation from standards are minimized and stated goals of the organization are achieved in desired manner. According to modern concepts, _____ is a foreseeing action whereas earlier concept of _____ was used only when errors were detected. _____ in management means setting standards, measuring actual performance and taking corrective action.
a. Decision tree pruning
b. Turnover
c. Schedule of reinforcement
d. Control

32. _____, commonly known as e-commerce, consists of the buying and selling of products or services over electronic systems such as the Internet and other computer networks. The amount of trade conducted electronically has grown extraordinarily with widespread Internet usage. The use of commerce is conducted in this way, spurring and drawing on innovations in electronic funds transfer, supply chain management, Internet marketing, online transaction processing, electronic data interchange (EDI), inventory management systems, and automated data collection systems.
a. A Stake in the Outcome
b. A4e
c. Online shopping
d. Electronic commerce

Chapter 11. Organizational Structure and Change

33. A _____ is a volunteer group composed of workers (or even students), usually under the leadership of their supervisor (but they can elect a team leader), who are trained to identify, analyse and solve work-related problems and present their solutions to management in order to improve the performance of the organization, and motivate and enrich the work of employees. When matured, true _____s become self-managing, having gained the confidence of management. _____s are an alternative to the dehumanising concept of the Division of Labour, where workers or individuals are treated like robots.

    a. Connectionist expert systems
    b. Certified in Production and Inventory Management
    c. Competency-based job descriptions
    d. Quality circle

34. In engineering and manufacturing, _____ and quality engineering are used in developing systems to ensure products or services are designed and produced to meet or exceed customer requirements. Refer to the definition by Merriam-Webster for further information . These systems are often developed in conjunction with other business and engineering disciplines using a cross-functional approach.

    a. Process capability
    b. Single Minute Exchange of Die
    c. Statistical process control
    d. Quality control

35. _____ is a process of gathering, analyzing, and dispensing information for tactical or strategic purposes. The _____ process entails obtaining both factual and subjective information on the business environments in which a company is operating or considering entering.

There are three ways of scanning the business environment:

- Ad-hoc scanning - Short term, infrequent examinations usually initiated by a crisis
- Regular scanning - Studies done on a regular schedule (say, once a year)
- Continuous scanning(also called continuous learning) - continuous structured data collection and processing on a broad range of environmental factors

Most commentators feel that in today's turbulent business environment the best scanning method available is continuous scanning. This allows the firm to :

-act quickly-take advantage of opportunities before competitors do-respond to environmental threats before significant damage is done

    a. AAAI
    b. A Stake in the Outcome
    c. Environmental scanning
    d. A4e

36. _____ is a layer of management in an organization whose primary job responsibility is to monitor activities of subordinates while reporting to upper management.

In pre-computer times, _____ would collect information from junior management and reassemble it for senior management. With the advent of inexpensive PCs this function has been taken over by e-business systems.

    a. Middle management
    b. Continuous monitoring
    c. Community management
    d. Theory Y

37. _____ is the life cycle of an organization from birth level to the termination.

Chapter 11. Organizational Structure and Change

There are five level/stages in any organization.

1. Birth
2. Growth
3. Maturity
4. Decline
5. Death

According to Richard L. Daft there are four stages in an _____.

The four stages are:

1. Entrepreneurial stage -> Crisis: Need for leadership
2. Collectivity stage -> Crisis: Need for delegation
3. Formalization stage -> Crisis: Too much red tape
4. Elaboration stage -> Crisis: Need for revitalization

(Richard L. Daft, Understanding the Theory and Design of Organizations, first edition 2007, ISBN 0-324-42271-7)

a. A4e
b. Organizational life cycle
c. A Stake in the Outcome
d. AAAI

38. _____ is a recursive process where two or more people or organizations work together in an intersection of common goals -- for example, an intellectual endeavor that is creative in nature--by sharing knowledge, learning and building consensus. _____ does not require leadership and can sometimes bring better results through decentralization and egalitarianism. In particular, teams that work collaboratively can obtain greater resources, recognition and reward when facing competition for finite resources. _____ is also present in opposing goals exhibiting the notion of adversarial _____, though this is not a common case for using the term.

a. 1990 Clean Air Act
b. Collectivism
c. Collaboration
d. 28-hour day

39. In decision theory and estimation theory, the _____ of an estimator, $\hat{\theta}$, of an unknown parameter of the distribution, θ, is the expected value of the loss function

$$R(\theta, \hat{\theta}) = \mathbb{E}_\theta L(\theta, \hat{\theta}) = \int L(\theta, \hat{\theta})\, dP_\theta.$$

Chapter 11. Organizational Structure and Change

where dP_θ is a probability measure parametrized by θ.

- For a scalar parameter θ and a quadratic loss function,

$$L(\theta, \hat{\theta}) = (\theta - \hat{\theta})^2$$

the _____ function becomes the mean squared error of the estimate,

$$R(\theta, \hat{\theta}) = E_\theta(\theta - \hat{\theta})^2$$

- In density estimation, the unknown parameter is probability density itself. The loss function is typically chosen to be a norm in an appropriate function space. For example, for L^2 norm,

$$L(f, \hat{f}) = \|f - \hat{f}\|_2^2$$

the _____ function becomes the mean integrated squared error

$$R(f, \hat{f}) = E\|f - \hat{f}\|^2$$

    a. Linear model   b. Risk
    c. Financial modeling   d. Risk aversion

40. _____ is an area of knowledge within organizational theory that studies models and theories about the way an organization learns and adapts.

In Organizational development (OD), learning is a characteristic of an adaptive organization, i.e., an organization that is able to sense changes in signals from its environment (both internal and external) and adapt accordingly.

    a. A4e   b. AAAI
    c. A Stake in the Outcome   d. Organizational learning

41. A _____ is a group of employees from various functional areas of the organization - research, engineering, marketing, finance. human resources, and operations, for example - who are all focused on a specific objective and are responsible to work as a team to improve coordination and innovation across divisions and resolve mutual problems.
    a. Sociotechnical systems   b. Goal-setting theory
    c. Graduate recruitment   d. Cross-functional team

42. As defined by Richard Beckhard, _____ is a planned, top-down, organization-wide effort to increase the organization's effectiveness and health. _____ is achieved through interventions in the organization's 'processes,' using behavioural science knowledge. According to Warren Bennis, _____ is a complex strategy intended to change the beliefs, attitudes, values, and structure of organizations so that they can better adapt to new technologies, markets, and challenges.

  a. Organizational structure
  b. Organizational culture
  c. Informal organization
  d. Organizational development

Chapter 12. Staffing

1. _____ refers to increasing the spiritual, political, social or economic strength of individuals and communities. It often involves the empowered developing confidence in their own capacities.

The term Human _____ covers a vast landscape of meanings, interpretations, definitions and disciplines ranging from psychology and philosophy to the highly commercialized Self-Help industry and Motivational sciences.

   a. Empowerment
   b. AAAI
   c. A4e
   d. A Stake in the Outcome

2. The term _____ collectively refers to all resources that determine the value and the competitiveness of an enterprise. As such, it includes as subsets the attributes that concur to building all financial statements as well as the balance sheet.
   a. AAAI
   b. A Stake in the Outcome
   c. A4e
   d. Intellectual capital

3. _____ is one of the managerial functions like planning, organizing, staffing and directing. It is an important function because it helps to check the errors and to take the corrective action so that deviation from standards are minimized and stated goals of the organization are achieved in desired manner.According to modern concepts, _____ is a foreseeing action whereas earlier concept of _____ was used only when errors were detected. _____ in management means setting standards, measuring actual performance and taking corrective action.
   a. Decision tree pruning
   b. Turnover
   c. Schedule of reinforcement
   d. Control

4. The U.S. _____ is an independent agency of the United States government which holds primary responsibility for enforcing the federal securities laws and regulating the securities industry, the nation's stock and options exchanges, and other electronic securities markets. The SEC was created by section 4 of the Securities Exchange Act of 1934 (now codified as 15 U.S.C. Â§ 78d and commonly referred to as the 1934 Act.)
   a. 1990 Clean Air Act
   b. 33 Strategies of War
   c. Securities and Exchange Commission
   d. 28-hour day

5. _____ is a method by which the job performance of an employee is evaluated _____ is a part of career development.

_____s are regular reviews of employee performance within organizations

Generally, the aims of a _____ are to:

- Give feedback on performance to employees.
- Identify employee training needs.
- Document criteria used to allocate organizational rewards.
- Form a basis for personnel decisions: salary increases, promotions, disciplinary actions, etc.
- Provide the opportunity for organizational diagnosis and development.
- Facilitate communication between employee and administraton
- Validate selection techniques and human resource policies to meet federal Equal Employment Opportunity requirements.

Chapter 12. Staffing

A common approach to assessing performance is to use a numerical or scalar rating system whereby managers are asked to score an individual against a number of objectives/attributes. In some companies, employees receive assessments from their manager, peers, subordinates and customers while also performing a self assessment.

    a. Personnel management   b. Human resource management
    c. Progressive discipline   d. Performance appraisal

6. In the field of human resource management, _____ is the field concerned with organizational activity aimed at bettering the performance of individuals and groups in organizational settings. It has been known by several names, including employee development, human resource development, and learning and development.

Harrison observes that the name was endlessly debated by the Chartered Institute of Personnel and Development during its review of professional standards in 1999/2000.

    a. Person specification   b. Training and development
    c. Revolving door syndrome   d. Performance appraisal

7. _____ is a contract between two parties, one being the employer and the other being the employee. An employee may be defined as: 'A person in the service of another under any contract of hire, express or implied, oral or written, where the employer has the power or right to control and direct the employee in the material details of how the work is to be performed.' Black's Law Dictionary page 471 (5th ed. 1979.)

    a. Employment   b. Employment rate
    c. Exit interview   d. Employment counsellor

8. The term _____ was created by President Lyndon B. Johnson when he signed Executive Order 11246 on September 24, 1965, created to prohibit federal contractors from discriminating against employees on the basis of race, sex, creed, religion, color, or national origin. In more recent times, most employers have also added sexual orientation to the list of non-discrimination.

The Executive Order also required contractors to implement affirmative action plans to increase the participation of minorities and women in the workplace.

    a. A Stake in the Outcome   b. A4e
    c. Equal Employment Opportunity   d. AAAI

9. The U.S. _____ is a federal agency whose goal is ending employment discrimination. The _____ investigates discrimination complaints based on an individual's race, color, national origin, religion, sex, age, disability and retaliation for reporting and/or opposing a discriminatory practice. The Commission is also tasked with filing suits on behalf of alleged victim(s) of discrimination against employers and as an adjudicatory for claims of discrimination brought against federal agencies.

    a. Airbus SAS   b. Airbus Industrie
    c. ARCO   d. Equal Employment Opportunity Commission

10. The _____ of 1990 (ADA) is the short title of United States (Pub.L. 101-336, 104 Stat. 327, enacted July 26, 1990), codified at 42 U.S.C. § 12101 et seq. It was signed into law on July 26, 1990, by President George H. W. Bush, and later amended with changes effective January 1, 2009. The ADA is a wide-ranging civil rights law that prohibits, under certain circumstances, discrimination based on disability. It affords similar protections against discrimination to Americans with disabilities as the Civil Rights Act of 1964,

a. Americans with Disabilities Act
b. Employment discrimination
c. Australian labour law
d. Equal Pay Act of 1963

11. The _____ is a United States statute that was passed in response to a series of United States Supreme Court decisions which limited the rights of employees who had sued their employers for discrimination. The Act represented the first effort since the passage of the Civil Rights Act of 1964 to modify some of the basic procedural and substantive rights provided by federal law in employment discrimination cases. It provided for the right to trial by jury on discrimination claims and introduced the possibility of emotional distress damages, while limiting the amount that a jury could award

The 1991 Act combined elements from two different civil rights acts of the past: the Civil Rights Act of 1866, better known by the number assigned to it in the codification of federal laws as 'Section 1981', and the employment-related provisions of the Civil Rights Act of 1964, generally referred to as 'Title VII', its location within the Act.

a. Negligence in employment
b. Resource Conservation and Recovery Act
c. Covenant
d. Civil Rights Act of 1991

12. The _____ 1970 is an Act of the United Kingdom Parliament which prohibits any less favourable treatment between men and women in terms of pay and conditions of employment. It came into force on 29 December 1975. The term pay is interpreted in a broad sense to include, on top of wages, things like holidays, pension rights, company perks and some kinds of bonuses.

a. Architectural Barriers Act of 1968
b. Australian labour law
c. Equal Pay Act
d. Oncale v. Sundowner Offshore Services

13. The _____, Pub. L. No. 88-38, 77 Stat. 56, (June 10, 1963) codified at 29 U.S.C. § 206(d), is a United States federal law amending the Fair Labor Standards Act, aimed at abolishing wage differentials based on sex. In passing the bill, Congress denounces sex discrimination.

a. Equal Pay Act of 1963
b. Extra time
c. Invitee
d. Architectural Barriers Act of 1968

14. _____ occurs when expectant women are fired, not hired, or otherwise discriminated against due to their pregnancy or intention to become pregnant. Common forms of _____ include not being hired due to visible pregnancy or likelihood of becoming pregnant, being fired after informing an employer of one's pregnancy, being fired after maternity leave, and receiving a pay dock due to pregnancy. In the United States, since 1978, employers are legally bound to provide what insurance, leave pay, and additional support that would be bestowed upon any employee with medical leave or disability.

a. 33 Strategies of War
b. 28-hour day
c. 1990 Clean Air Act
d. Pregnancy Discrimination

Chapter 12. Staffing

15. The _____, 5 U.S.C. § 552a, establishes a code of fair information practices that governs the collection, maintenance, use, and dissemination of personally identifiable information about individuals that is maintained in systems of records by federal agencies. A system of records is a group of records under the control of an agency from which information is retrieved by the name of the individual or by some identifier assigned to the individual.
   a. Negligence
   b. No-FEAR Act
   c. Personal Responsibility and Work Opportunity Reconciliation Act
   d. Privacy Act of 1974

16. The U.S. _____ of 1973 prohibits discrimination on the basis of disability in programs conducted by Federal agencies, in programs receiving Federal financial assistance, in Federal employment, and in the employment practices of Federal contractors. The standards for determining employment discrimination under the _____ are the same as those used in title I of the Americans with Disabilities Act.

There are four key sections of the Act.

   a. 33 Strategies of War
   b. 28-hour day
   c. Rehabilitation Act
   d. 1990 Clean Air Act

17. _____ is the point where a person stops employment completely. A person may also semi-retire and keep some sort of _____ job, out of choice rather than necessity. This usually happens upon reaching a determined age, when physical conditions don't allow the person to work any more (by illness or accident), or even for personal choice (usually in the presence of an adequate pension or personal savings.)
   a. Retirement
   b. Termination of employment
   c. Wrongful dismissal
   d. Severance package

18. _____ is unwelcome harassment of a sexual nature, or based upon the receiving party's sex or gender. In some contexts or circumstances, _____ may be illegal. It includes a range of behavior from seemingly mild transgressions and annoyances to actual sexual abuse or sexual assault.
   a. Sexual Harassment
   b. 1990 Clean Air Act
   c. 28-hour day
   d. Hypernorms

19. In employment law, a (BFOQ) (US) or bona fide occupational requirement (BFOR) (Canada) is a quality or an attribute that employers are allowed to consider when making decisions on the hiring and retention of employees - qualities that, when considered, in other contexts would be considered discriminatory and thus violating civil rights employment law.

In employment discrimination law in the United States, United States Code Title 29 , Chapter 14 (age discrimination in employment), section 623 (prohibition of age discrimination) establishes that 'It shall not be unlawful for an employer, employment agency, or labor organization (1) to take any action otherwise prohibited under subsections (a), (b), (c), or (e) of this section where age is a _____ reasonably necessary to the normal operation of the particular business, or where the differentiation is based on reasonable factors other than age, or where such practices involve an employee in a workplace in a foreign country, and compliance with such subsections would cause such employer, or a corporation controlled by such employer, to violate the laws of the country in which such workplace is located.'

One example of _____s are mandatory retirement ages for bus drivers and airline pilots, for safety reasons. Further, in advertising, a manufacturer of men's clothing may lawfully advertise for male models.

a. MacPherson v. Buick Motor Co.
b. Sick leave
c. Corporate governance
d. Bona fide occupational qualification

20. _____ is the concept of a person or group of people being in charge or in command of another person or group. This control is often granted to the senior person(s) due to experience or length of service in a given position, but it is not uncommon for a senior person(s) to have less experience or length of service than their subordinates.

More generally, '_____' can be a description of an individual's experience or length of service, and can thus be used to differentiate between individuals of otherwise equivalent status without placing them in a hierarchy of direct authority.

a. 28-hour day
b. 1990 Clean Air Act
c. 33 Strategies of War
d. Seniority

21. A _____ is typically described as a deliberate plan of action to guide decisions and achieve rational outcome(s.) However, the term may also be used to denote what is actually done, even though it is unplanned.

The term may apply to government, private sector organizations and groups, and individuals.

a. Policy
b. 1990 Clean Air Act
c. 33 Strategies of War
d. 28-hour day

22. _____ is an advertisement in which a particular product specifically mentions a competitor by name for the express purpose of showing why the competitor is inferior to the product naming it.

This should not be confused with parody advertisements, where a fictional product is being advertised for the purpose of poking fun at the particular advertisement, nor should it be confused with the use of a coined brand name for the purpose of comparing the product without actually naming an actual competitor. ('Wikipedia tastes better and is less filling than the Encyclopedia Galactica.')

In the 1980s, during what has been referred to as the cola wars, soft-drink manufacturer Pepsi ran a series of advertisements where people, caught on hidden camera, in a blind taste test, chose Pepsi over rival Coca-Cola.

a. 1990 Clean Air Act
b. 28-hour day
c. 33 Strategies of War
d. Comparative advertising

23.

The terms _____ and positive action refer to policies that take race, ethnicity, or gender into consideration in an attempt to promote equal opportunity. The focus of such policies ranges from employment and education to public contracting and health programs. The impetus towards _____ is twofold: to maximize diversity in all levels of society, along with its presumed benefits, and to redress perceived disadvantages due to overt, institutional, or involuntary discrimination.

a. Affirmative action
b. Abraham Harold Maslow
c. Affiliation
d. Adam Smith

24. In US employment law, _____ is defined as a substantially different rate of selection in hiring, promotion sex statistical significance tests, and/or practical significance tests. _____ is often used interchangeably with 'disparate impact,' which was a legal term coined in one of the most significant U.S. Supreme Court rulings on disparate or _____: Griggs v. Duke Power Co., 1971.

a. A Stake in the Outcome
b. A4e
c. AAAI
d. Adverse impact

25. In economics, the people in the _____ are the suppliers of labor. The _____ is all the nonmilitary people who are employed or unemployed. In 2005, the worldwide _____ was over 3 billion people.

a. Labor force
b. Pink-collar worker
c. Departmentalization
d. Decent work

26. In game theory, an _____ is a set of moves or strategies taken by the players, or their payoffs resulting from the actions or strategies taken by all players. The two are complementary in that given knowledge of the set of strategies of all players, the final state of the game is known, as are any relevant payoffs. In a game where chance or a random event is involved, the _____ is not known from only the set of strategies, but is only realized when the random event(s) are realized.

a. A Stake in the Outcome
b. A4e
c. AAAI
d. Outcome

27. The 'business case for _____', theorizes that in a global marketplace, a company that employs a diverse workforce (both men and women, people of many generations, people from ethnically and racially diverse backgrounds etc.) is better able to understand the demographics of the marketplace it serves and is thus better equipped to thrive in that marketplace than a company that has a more limited range of employee demographics.

An additional corollary suggests that a company that supports the _____ of its workforce can also improve employee satisfaction, productivity and retention.

a. Virtual team
b. Diversity
c. Trademark
d. Kanban

28. In economics, the term _____ refers to situations where the advancement of a qualified person within the hierarchy of an organization is stopped at a lower level because of some form of discrimination, most commonly sexism or racism, but since the term was coined, '_____' has also come to describe the limited advancement of the deaf, blind, disabled, aged and sexual minorities. It is an unofficial, invisible barrier that prevents women and minorities from advancing in businesses.

This situation is referred to as a 'ceiling' as there is a limitation blocking upward advancement, and 'glass' (transparent) because the limitation is not immediately apparent and is normally an unwritten and unofficial policy. This invisible barrier continues to exist, even though there are no explicit obstacles keeping minorities from acquiring advanced job positions - there are no advertisements that specifically say 'no minorities hired at this establishment', nor are there any formal orders that say 'minorities are not qualified' - but they do lie beneath the surface.

Chapter 12. Staffing

a. 1990 Clean Air Act
b. 28-hour day
c. 33 Strategies of War
d. Glass Ceiling

29. _____ are conventions, treaties and recommendations designed to eliminate unjust and inhumane labour practices. The primary inernational agency charged with developing such standards is the International Labour Organization (ILO.) Established in 1919, the ILO advocates international standards as essential for the eradication of labour conditions involving 'injustice, hardship and privation'.

a. Anaconda Copper
b. International labour standards
c. Airbus Industrie
d. Airbus SAS

30. _____ is a mathematical science pertaining to the collection, analysis, interpretation or explanation, and presentation of data. It also provides tools for prediction and forecasting based on data. It is applicable to a wide variety of academic disciplines, from the natural and social sciences to the humanities, government and business.

a. Statistics
b. Simple moving average
c. Failure rate
d. Location parameter

31. In organized labor, _____ is the method whereby workers organize together (usually in unions) to meet, converse, and negotiate upon the work conditions with their employers normally resulting in a written contract setting forth the wages, hours, and other conditions to be observed for a stipulated period.It is the practice in which union and company representatives meet to negotiate a new labor contract. In various national labor and employment law contexts, the term _____ takes on a more specific legal meaning. In a broad sense, however, it is the coming together of workers to negotiate their employment.

a. Collective bargaining
b. Labor rights
c. Paid time off
d. Labour law

32. An arbitral tribunal (or arbitration tribunal) is a panel of one or more adjudicators which is convened and sits to resolve a dispute by way of arbitration. The tribunal may consist of a sole _____, or there may be two or more _____s, which might include either a chairman or an umpire. The parties to a dispute are usually free to agree the number and composition of the arbitral tribunal.

a. A4e
b. AAAI
c. A Stake in the Outcome
d. Arbitrator

33. _____ refers to various methodologies for analyzing the requirements of a job.

The general purpose of _____ is to document the requirements of a job and the work performed. Job and task analysis is performed as a basis for later improvements, including: definition of a job domain; describing a job; developing performance appraisals, selection systems, promotion criteria, training needs assessment, and compensation plans.

a. Hersey-Blanchard situational theory
b. Job analysis
c. Management process
d. Work design

34. A _____ is a list of the general tasks and responsibilities of a position. Typically, it also includes to whom the position reports, specifications such as the qualifications needed by the person in the job, salary range for the position, etc. A _____ is usually developed by conducting a job analysis, which includes examining the tasks and sequences of tasks necessary to perform the job.

Chapter 12. Staffing

  a. Job description
  b. Recruitment advertising
  c. Recruitment
  d. Recruitment Process Insourcing

35. _____ is the process of estimation in unknown situations. Prediction is a similar, but more general term. Both can refer to estimation of time series, cross-sectional or longitudinal data.
  a. Forecasting
  b. 33 Strategies of War
  c. 1990 Clean Air Act
  d. 28-hour day

36. _____ is execution of a series of programs ('jobs') on a computer without human interaction.

Batch jobs are set up so they can be run to completion without human interaction, so all input data is preselected through scripts or command-line parameters. This is in contrast to 'online' or interactive programs which prompt the user for such input.

  a. 1990 Clean Air Act
  b. 28-hour day
  c. 33 Strategies of War
  d. Batch processing

37. _____ is the strategic and coherent approach to the management of an organisation's most valued assets - the people working there who individually and collectively contribute to the achievement of the objectives of the business. The terms '_____' and 'human resources' (HR) have largely replaced the term 'personnel management' as a description of the processes involved in managing people in organizations. In simple sense, _____ means employing people, developing their resources, utilizing, maintaining and compensating their services in tune with the job and organizational requirement.
  a. Job knowledge
  b. Revolving door syndrome
  c. Progressive discipline
  d. Human Resource Management

38. _____ is a cross-disciplinary area concerned with protecting the safety, health and welfare of people engaged in work or employment. The goal of all _____ programs is to foster a work free safe environment. As a secondary effect, it may also protect co-workers, family members, employers, customers, suppliers, nearby communities, and other members of the public who are impacted by the workplace environment.
  a. Occupational Safety and Health
  b. A Stake in the Outcome
  c. A4e
  d. AAAI

39. The United States _____ is an agency of the United States Department of Labor. It was created by Congress under the Occupational Safety and Health Act, signed by President Richard M. Nixon, on December 29, 1970. Its mission is to prevent work-related injuries, illnesses, and deaths by issuing and enforcing rules (called standards) for workplace safety and health.
  a. Occupational Safety and Health Administration
  b. Opinion leadership
  c. Operant conditioning
  d. Unemployment insurance

40. A _____ or background investigation is the process of looking up and compiling criminal records, commercial records and financial records (in certain instances such as employment screening) of an individual.

Chapter 12. Staffing

_____s are often requested by employers on job candidates, especially on candidates seeking a position that requires high security or a position of trust, such as in a school, hospital, financial institution, airport, and government (including law enforcement and military.) These checks are traditionally administered by a government agency for a nominal fee, but can also be administered by private companies.

- a. Time and attendance
- b. Background check
- c. Malcolm Baldrige National Quality Award
- d. Labour productivity

41. _____ is an integrated communications-based process through which individuals and communities discover that existing and newly-identified needs and wants may be satisfied by the products and services of others.

_____ is defined by the American _____ Association as the activity, set of institutions, and processes for creating, communicating, delivering, and exchanging offerings that have value for customers, clients, partners, and society at large. The term developed from the original meaning which referred literally to going to market, as in shopping, or going to a market to buy or sell goods or services.

- a. Customer relationship management
- b. Disruptive technology
- c. Market development
- d. Marketing

42. _____ is a form of marketing developed from direct response marketing campaigns conducted in the 1970s and 1980s which emphasizes customer retention and satisfaction, rather than a dominant focus on point-of-sale transactions.

_____ differs from other forms of marketing in that it recognizes the long term value to the firm of keeping customers, as opposed to direct or 'Intrusion' marketing, which focuses upon acquisition of new clients by targeting majority demographics based upon prospective client lists.

_____ refers to a long-term and mutually beneficial arrangement wherein both the buyer and seller focus on value enhancement with the goal of providing a more satisfying exchange.

- a. 28-hour day
- b. Guerrilla marketing
- c. Relationship Marketing
- d. 1990 Clean Air Act

43. The _____ is a Cabinet department of the United States government responsible for occupational safety, wage and hour standards, unemployment insurance benefits, re-employment services, and some economic statistics. Many U.S. states also have such departments. The department is headed by the United States Secretary of Labor.
- a. A Stake in the Outcome
- b. United States Department of Labor
- c. AAAI
- d. A4e

44. A _____ is a group of employees from various functional areas of the organization - research, engineering, marketing, finance. human resources, and operations, for example - who are all focused on a specific objective and are responsible to work as a team to improve coordination and innovation across divisions and resolve mutual problems.
- a. Cross-functional team
- b. Sociotechnical systems
- c. Graduate recruitment
- d. Goal-setting theory

Chapter 12. Staffing

45. _____ is a management technique pioneered by Michael Phillips in San Francisco in the late '60's and early '70s. The concept's most visible success was by Jack Stack and his team at SRC Holdings and popularized in 1995 by John Case. The technique is to give employees all relevant financial information about the company so they can make better decisions as workers.

   a. A Stake in the Outcome
   b. A4e
   c. AAAI
   d. Open-book management

46. _____ is an approach to management development where an individual is moved through a schedule of assignments designed to give him or her a breadth of exposure to the entire operation.

   _____ is also practiced to allow qualified employees to gain more insights into the processes of a company, and to reduce boredom and increase job satisfaction through job variation.

   The term _____ can also mean the scheduled exchange of persons in offices, especially in public offices, prior to the end of incumbency or the legislative period.

   a. 33 Strategies of War
   b. 28-hour day
   c. 1990 Clean Air Act
   d. Job rotation

47. There are two types of _____ relationships: formal and informal. Informal relationships develop on their own between partners. Formal _____, on the other hand, refers to assigned relationships, often associated with organizational _____ programs designed to promote employee development or to assist at-risk children and youth.

   a. Mentoring
   b. Fix it twice
   c. Human resource management system
   d. Real Property Administrator

48. In psychology research on behaviorism, _____ are scales used to report performance. _____ are normally presented vertically with scale points ranging from five to nine.

   It is an appraisal method that aims to combine the benefits of narratives, critical incident incidents, and quantified ratings by anchoring a quantified scale with specific narrative examples of good or poor performance.

   a. 1990 Clean Air Act
   b. 28-hour day
   c. 33 Strategies of War
   d. Behaviorally anchored rating scales

49. A _____ is a set of categories designed to elicit information about a quantitative or a qualitative attribute. In the social sciences, common examples are the Likert scale and 1-10 _____s in which a person selects the number which is considered to reflect the perceived quality of a product.

   A _____ is an instrument that requires the rater to assign the rated object that have numerals assigned to them.

   a. Spearman-Brown prediction formula
   b. Polytomous Rasch model
   c. Rating scale
   d. Thurstone scale

50. _____ is a form of communication that typically attempts to persuade potential customers to purchase or to consume more of a particular brand of product or service. 'While now central to the contemporary global economy and the reproduction of global production networks, it is only quite recently that _____ has been more than a marginal influence on patterns of sales and production. The formation of modern _____ was intimately bound up with the emergence of new forms of monopoly capitalism around the end of the 19th and beginning of the 20th century as one element in corporate strategies to create, organize and where possible control markets, especially for mass produced consumer goods.

   a. AAAI
   b. A4e
   c. A Stake in the Outcome
   d. Advertising

51. _____ describes the situation when output from (or information about the result of) an event or phenomenon in the past will influence the same event/phenomenon in the present or future. When an event is part of a chain of cause-and-effect that forms a circuit or loop, then the event is said to 'feed back' into itself.

_____ is also a synonym for:

- _____ signal; the information about the initial event that is the basis for subsequent modification of the event.
- _____ loop; the causal path that leads from the initial generation of the _____ signal to the subsequent modification of the event.

_____ is a mechanism, process or signal that is looped back to control a system within itself. Such a loop is called a _____ loop.

   a. Feedback
   b. Positive feedback
   c. 1990 Clean Air Act
   d. Feedback loop

52. _____ is a term defined by the Oxford English Dictionary as an individual's 'course or progress through life '. It is usually considered to pertain to remunerative work (and sometimes also formal education.)

The etymology of the term is somewhat ironic in that it comes from the Latin word carrera, which means race .

   a. Career planning
   b. Career
   c. Spatial mismatch
   d. Nursing shortage

53. _____ has been described as the 'process of social influence in which one person can enlist the aid and support of others in the accomplishment of a common task' . A definition more inclusive of followers comes from Alan Keith of Genentech who said '_____ is ultimately about creating a way for people to contribute to making something extraordinary happen.'

_____ is one of the most salient aspects of the organizational context. However, defining _____ has been challenging.

   a. Situational leadership
   b. Leadership
   c. 1990 Clean Air Act
   d. 28-hour day

Chapter 12. Staffing

54. An _____ is a person who has possession of an enterprise and assumes significant accountability for the inherent risks and the outcome. It is an ambitious leader who combines land, labor, and capital to create and market new goods or services. The term is a loanword from French and was first defined by the Irish economist Richard Cantillon.
    a. A4e
    b. Entrepreneur
    c. AAAI
    d. A Stake in the Outcome

55. _____ is a term used to describe the lifestyle of women who choose to leave the workforce (typically in white collar career positions) in order to pursue childbearing. This is the converse of the Fast Track, where one devotes considerable energy to career building.

This is a source of considerable political and social discussion.

    a. 33 Strategies of War
    b. 1990 Clean Air Act
    c. 28-hour day
    d. Mommy track

56. _____ is the process of recruiting individuals to fill executive positions in organizations. _____ may be performed by an organization's board of directors, by executives in the organization, or by an outside _____ organization.

The _____ profession has two distinct fields, retained _____ and contingency search.

    a. Internet recruiting
    b. Employee referral
    c. Employment agency
    d. Executive Search

57. An _____ is an interview conducted by an employer of a departing employee. They are generally conducted by a relatively neutral party, such as a human resources staff member, so that the employee will be more inclined to be candid, as opposed to worrying about burning bridges. For this reason, some companies opt to employ a third party to conduct the interviews and provide feedback.
    a. Exit interview
    b. Extra role performance
    c. Occupational Employment Statistics
    d. Underemployment

58. The _____ of 1938 (_____, ch. 676, 52 Stat. 1060, June 25, 1938, 29 U.S.C. ch.8), also called the Wages and Hours Bill, is United States federal law that applies to employees engaged in interstate commerce or employed by an enterprise engaged in commerce or in the production of goods for commerce, unless the employer can claim an exemption from coverage. The _____ established a national minimum wage, guaranteed time and a half for overtime in certain jobs, and prohibited most employment of minors in 'oppressive child labor,' a term defined in the statute.
    a. Family and Medical Leave Act of 1993
    b. Joint venture
    c. Board of directors
    d. Fair Labor Standards Act

Chapter 12. Staffing

59. _____ is the process of systematically determining a relative value of jobs in an organisation. In all cases the idea is to evaluate the job, not the person doing it.

- Job Ranking is the most simple form. Basically you just order the jobs according to perceived seniority. It's easy in a small organization, but get exponentially difficult with lots of different jobs.

- Pair Comparison introduces more rigour by comparing jobs in pairs, but really it's a more structured way of building a basic rank order.

- Benchmarking or slotting sets up certain jobs that are analysed in detail. These are then used for comparison to slot jobs against these benchmarks.

a. 1990 Clean Air Act
b. 28-hour day
c. 33 Strategies of War
d. Job evaluation

60. _____ occurs when a person is available to work and seeking work but currently without work. The prevalence of _____ is usually measured using the _____ rate, which is defined as the percentage of those in the labor force who are unemployed. The _____ rate is also used in economic studies and economic indexes such as the United States' Conference Board's Index of Leading Indicators as a measure of the state of the macroeconomics.

a. Employment-to-population ratio
b. Unemployment
c. Unemployment Convention, 1919
d. Outplacement

61. _____ is money received by an unemployed worker from the United States or a state. In the United States, this compensation is classified as a type of social welfare benefit. According to the Internal Revenue Code, these types of benefits are to be included in a taxpayer's gross income.

a. Unemployment
b. Unemployment insurance
c. Unemployment Provision Convention, 1934
d. Unemployment compensation

62. In finance, an _____ is a contract between a buyer and a seller that gives the buyer the right--but not the obligation--to buy or to sell a particular asset (the underlying asset) at a later day at an agreed price. In return for granting the _____, the seller collects a payment (the premium) from the buyer. A call _____ gives the buyer the right to buy the underlying asset; a put _____ gives the buyer of the _____ the right to sell the underlying asset.

a. A Stake in the Outcome
b. A4e
c. AAAI
d. Option

63. In human resources or industrial/organizational psychology, _____ ' 'multisource feedback,' or 'multisource assessment,' is feedback that comes from all around an employee. '360' refers to the 360 degrees in a circle, with an individual figuratively in the center of the circle. Feedback is provided by subordinates, peers, and supervisors.

a. Personnel management
b. Revolving door syndrome
c. Job knowledge
d. 360-degree feedback

64. _____ refers to the aggregated strategies of single business firm or a strategic business unit (SBU) in a diversified corporation. According to Michael Porter, a firm must formulate a _____ that incorporates either cost leadership, differentiation or focus in order to achieve a sustainable competitive advantage and long-term success in its chosen arenas or industries.

Functional strategies include marketing strategies, new product development strategies, human resource strategies, financial strategies, legal strategies, supply-chain strategies, and information technology management strategies.

a. Competitive heterogeneity
b. Switching cost
c. Strategic thinking
d. Business strategy

Chapter 13. Communication: Interpersonal and Organizational

1. _____ is the provision of service to customers before, during and after a purchase.

According to Turban et al. (2002), '_____ is a series of activities designed to enhance the level of customer satisfaction - that is, the feeling that a product or service has met the customer expectation.'

Its importance varies by product, industry and customer; defective or broken merchandise can be exchanged, often only with a receipt and within a specified time frame.

   a. Service rate
   b. 28-hour day
   c. 1990 Clean Air Act
   d. Customer service

2. _____ is an advertisement in which a particular product specifically mentions a competitor by name for the express purpose of showing why the competitor is inferior to the product naming it.

This should not be confused with parody advertisements, where a fictional product is being advertised for the purpose of poking fun at the particular advertisement, nor should it be confused with the use of a coined brand name for the purpose of comparing the product without actually naming an actual competitor. ('Wikipedia tastes better and is less filling than the Encyclopedia Galactica.')

In the 1980s, during what has been referred to as the cola wars, soft-drink manufacturer Pepsi ran a series of advertisements where people, caught on hidden camera, in a blind taste test, chose Pepsi over rival Coca-Cola.

   a. Comparative advertising
   b. 1990 Clean Air Act
   c. 28-hour day
   d. 33 Strategies of War

3. The _____ was a period in the late 18th and early 19th centuries when major changes in agriculture, manufacturing, mining, and transportation had a profound effect on the socioeconomic and cultural conditions in Britain. The changes subsequently spread throughout Europe, North America, and eventually the world. The onset of the _____ marked a major turning point in human society; almost every aspect of daily life was eventually influenced in some way.

   a. Abraham Harold Maslow
   b. Adam Smith
   c. Industrial Revolution
   d. Affiliation

4. _____ is a form of applied ethics that examines ethical principles and moral or ethical problems that arise in a business environment. It applies to all aspects of business conduct and is relevant to the conduct of individuals and business organizations as a whole. Applied ethics is a field of ethics that deals with ethical questions in many fields such as medical, technical, legal and _____.

   a. Hypernorms
   b. Facilitation payments
   c. Business Ethics
   d. Corporate Sustainability

5. _____ is a process of planning and controlling the performance or execution of any type of activity, such as:

   - a project (project _____) or
   - a process (process _____, sometimes referred to as the process performance measurement and management system.)

Organization's senior management is responsible for carrying out its _____.

Chapter 13. Communication: Interpersonal and Organizational

   a. Work design
   c. Participatory management
   b. Human Relations Movement
   d. Management process

6. _____ describes the situation when output from (or information about the result of) an event or phenomenon in the past will influence the same event/phenomenon in the present or future. When an event is part of a chain of cause-and-effect that forms a circuit or loop, then the event is said to 'feed back' into itself.

_____ is also a synonym for:

- _____ signal; the information about the initial event that is the basis for subsequent modification of the event.
- _____ loop; the causal path that leads from the initial generation of the _____ signal to the subsequent modification of the event.

_____ is a mechanism, process or signal that is looped back to control a system within itself. Such a loop is called a _____ loop.

   a. Feedback loop
   c. Feedback
   b. 1990 Clean Air Act
   d. Positive feedback

7. A _____ is a business that is privately owned and operated, with a small number of employees and relatively low volume of sales. The legal definition of 'small' often varies by country and industry, but is generally under 100 employees in the United States and under 50 employees in the European Union. In comparison, the definition of mid-sized business by the number of employees is generally under 500 in the U.S. and 250 for the European Union.
   a. Critical Success Factor
   c. Golden Boot Compensation
   b. Pre-determined overhead rate
   d. Small Business

8. The _____ is a United States government agency that provides support to small businesses.

The mission of the _____ is 'to maintain and strengthen the nation's economy by enabling the establishment and viability of small businesses and by assisting in the economic recovery of communities after disasters.'

The _____ makes loans directly to businesses and acts as a guarantor on bank loans. In some circumstances it also makes loans to victims of natural disasters, works to get government procurement contracts for small businesses, and assists businesses with management, technical and training issues.

   a. 1990 Clean Air Act
   c. 33 Strategies of War
   b. Small Business Administration
   d. 28-hour day

9. _____ is one of the managerial functions like planning, organizing, staffing and directing. It is an important function because it helps to check the errors and to take the corrective action so that deviation from standards are minimized and stated goals of the organization are achieved in desired manner. According to modern concepts, _____ is a foreseeing action whereas earlier concept of _____ was used only when errors were detected. _____ in management means setting standards, measuring actual performance and taking corrective action.

a. Decision tree pruning
c. Schedule of reinforcement
b. Control
d. Turnover

10. _____ is a form of communication that typically attempts to persuade potential customers to purchase or to consume more of a particular brand of product or service. 'While now central to the contemporary global economy and the reproduction of global production networks, it is only quite recently that _____ has been more than a marginal influence on patterns of sales and production. The formation of modern _____ was intimately bound up with the emergence of new forms of monopoly capitalism around the end of the 19th and beginning of the 20th century as one element in corporate strategies to create, organize and where possible control markets, especially for mass produced consumer goods.
- a. A4e
- b. AAAI
- c. A Stake in the Outcome
- d. Advertising

11. A _____ is directly responsible for managing the day-to-day operations (and profitability) of a company.

Chief Executive Officer (CEO)
- As the top manager, the CEO is typically responsible for the entire operations of the corporation and reports directly to the chairman and board of directors. It is the CEO's responsibility to implement board decisions and initiatives and to maintain the smooth operation of the firm, with the assistance of senior management.

- a. Vorstand
- b. Field service management
- c. Getting Things Done
- d. Management team

12. _____, widely known as F. W. Taylor, was an American mechanical engineer who sought to improve industrial efficiency. He is regarded as the father of scientific management, and was one of the first management consultants.

Taylor was one of the intellectual leaders of the Efficiency Movement and his ideas, broadly conceived, were highly influential in the Progressive Era.

- a. Geoffrey Colvin
- b. Jonah Jacob Goldberg
- c. Douglas N. Daft
- d. Frederick Winslow Taylor

13. _____ is a group creativity technique designed to generate a large number of ideas for the solution of a problem. The method was first popularized in the late 1930s by Alex Faickney Osborn in a book called Applied Imagination. Osborn proposed that groups could double their creative output with _____.
- a. Brainstorming
- b. Affiliation
- c. Abraham Harold Maslow
- d. Adam Smith

14. _____ is a method by which the job performance of an employee is evaluated _____ is a part of career development.

_____s are regular reviews of employee performance within organizations

Chapter 13. Communication: Interpersonal and Organizational

Generally, the aims of a _____ are to:

- Give feedback on performance to employees.
- Identify employee training needs.
- Document criteria used to allocate organizational rewards.
- Form a basis for personnel decisions: salary increases, promotions, disciplinary actions, etc.
- Provide the opportunity for organizational diagnosis and development.
- Facilitate communication between employee and administraton
- Validate selection techniques and human resource policies to meet federal Equal Employment Opportunity requirements.

A common approach to assessing performance is to use a numerical or scalar rating system whereby managers are asked to score an individual against a number of objectives/attributes. In some companies, employees receive assessments from their manager, peers, subordinates and customers while also performing a self assessment.

a. Progressive discipline
b. Human resource management
c. Personnel management
d. Performance appraisal

15. A _____ is a volunteer group composed of workers (or even students), usually under the leadership of their supervisor (but they can elect a team leader), who are trained to identify, analyse and solve work-related problems and present their solutions to management in order to improve the performance of the organization, and motivate and enrich the work of employees. When matured, true _____s become self-managing, having gained the confidence of management.
_____s are an alternative to the dehumanising concept of the Division of Labour, where workers or individuals are treated like robots.

a. Certified in Production and Inventory Management
b. Connectionist expert systems
c. Competency-based job descriptions
d. Quality circle

16. The 'business case for _____', theorizes that in a global marketplace, a company that employs a diverse workforce (both men and women, people of many generations, people from ethnically and racially diverse backgrounds etc.) is better able to understand the demographics of the marketplace it serves and is thus better equipped to thrive in that marketplace than a company that has a more limited range of employee demographics.

An additional corollary suggests that a company that supports the _____ of its workforce can also improve employee satisfaction, productivity and retention.

a. Kanban
b. Trademark
c. Virtual team
d. Diversity

17. In sociology, anthropology and cultural studies, a _____ is a group of people with a culture (whether distinct or hidden) which differentiates them from the larger culture to which they belong. If a particular _____ is characterized by a systematic opposition to the dominant culture, it may be described as a counterculture.

As early as 1950, David Riesman distinguished between a majority, 'which passively accepted commercially provided styles and meanings, and a '_____' which actively sought a minority style ...

Chapter 13. Communication: Interpersonal and Organizational

a. 28-hour day
b. 33 Strategies of War
c. 1990 Clean Air Act
d. Subculture

18. _____ is a subfield of the larger discipline of communication studies. _____, as a field, is the consideration, analysis, and criticism of the role of communication in organizational contexts.

The field traces its lineage through business information, business communication, and early mass communication studies published in the 1930s through the 1950s.

a. A4e
b. A Stake in the Outcome
c. AAAI
d. Organizational communication

19. In a military context, the _____ is the line of authority and responsibility along which orders are passed within a military unit and between different units. The term is also used in a civilian management context describing comparable hierarchical structures of authority.

a. French leave
b. 28-hour day
c. 1990 Clean Air Act
d. Chain of command

20. An _____, or organogram(me)) is a diagram that shows the structure of an organization and the relationships and relative ranks of its parts and positions/jobs. The term is also used for similar diagrams, for example ones showing the different elements of a field of knowledge or a group of languages. The French Encyclopédie had one of the first _____s of knowledge in general.

a. A4e
b. AAAI
c. A Stake in the Outcome
d. Organizational chart

21. In economics, the people in the _____ are the suppliers of labor. The _____ is all the nonmilitary people who are employed or unemployed. In 2005, the worldwide _____ was over 3 billion people.

a. Departmentalization
b. Pink-collar worker
c. Decent work
d. Labor force

22. _____ has been described as the 'process of social influence in which one person can enlist the aid and support of others in the accomplishment of a common task' . A definition more inclusive of followers comes from Alan Keith of Genentech who said '_____ is ultimately about creating a way for people to contribute to making something extraordinary happen.'

_____ is one of the most salient aspects of the organizational context. However, defining _____ has been challenging.

a. Situational leadership
b. 28-hour day
c. Leadership
d. 1990 Clean Air Act

23. _____ is a term originating in military organization theory, but now used more commonly in business management, particularly human resource management. _____ refers to the number of subordinates a supervisor has.

In the hierarchical business organization of the past it was not uncommon to see average spans of 1 to 10 or even less. That is, one manager supervised ten employees on average.

a. Senior management
c. Mentoring
b. Span of control
d. CIFMS

24. An _____ is a private computer network that uses Internet technologies to securely share any part of an organization's information or operational systems with its employees. Sometimes the term refers only to the organization's internal website, but often it is a more extensive part of the organization's computer infrastructure and private websites are an important component and focal point of internal communication and collaboration.

An _____ is built from the same concepts and technologies used for the Internet, such as client-server computing and the Internet Protocol Suite (TCP/IP.)

a. A Stake in the Outcome
c. Intranet
b. A4e
d. AAAI

Chapter 14. Human Motivation

1. Maslow's _____ is a theory in psychology, proposed by Abraham Maslow in his 1943 paper A Theory of Human Motivation, which he subsequently extended to include his observations of humans' innate curiosity.

   Maslow's _____ is predetermined in order of importance. It is often depicted as a pyramid consisting of five levels: the lowest level is associated with physiological needs, while the uppermost level is associated with self-actualization needs, particularly those related to identity and purpose. Deficiency needs must be met first. Once these are met, seeking to satisfy growth needs drives personal growth. The higher needs in this hierarchy only come into focus when the lower needs in the pyramid are met.

   a. 28-hour day
   b. 1990 Clean Air Act
   c. 33 Strategies of War
   d. Hierarchy of needs

2. _____ are job factors that can cause dissatisfaction if missing but do not necessarily motivate employees if increased.

   _____ have mostly to do with the job environment. These factors are important or notable only when they are lacking.

   a. Work-at-home scheme
   b. Work system
   c. Split shift
   d. Hygiene factors

3. _____ was developed by Frederick Herzberg, a psychologist who found that job satisfaction and job dissatisfaction acted independently of each other. _____ states that there are certain factors in the workplace that cause job satisfaction, while a separate set of factors cause dissatisfaction.

   a. 1990 Clean Air Act
   b. Need for power
   c. Need for Achievement
   d. Two-factor theory

4. _____ refers to increasing the spiritual, political, social or economic strength of individuals and communities. It often involves the empowered developing confidence in their own capacities.

   The term Human _____ covers a vast landscape of meanings, interpretations, definitions and disciplines ranging from psychology and philosophy to the highly commercialized Self-Help industry and Motivational sciences.

   a. AAAI
   b. A4e
   c. A Stake in the Outcome
   d. Empowerment

5. _____ is the practice of using entrepreneurial skills without taking on the risks or accountability associated with entrepreneurial activities. It is practiced by employees within an established organization using a business model. Employees, perhaps engaged in a special project within a larger firm are supposed to behave as entrepreneurs, even though they have the resources and capabilities of the larger firm to draw upon.

   a. A4e
   b. A Stake in the Outcome
   c. AAAI
   d. Intrapreneurship

6. A _____ is directly responsible for managing the day-to-day operations (and profitability) of a company.

Chapter 14. Human Motivation

Chief Executive Officer (CEO)
- As the top manager, the CEO is typically responsible for the entire operations of the corporation and reports directly to the chairman and board of directors. It is the CEO's responsibility to implement board decisions and initiatives and to maintain the smooth operation of the firm, with the assistance of senior management.

a. Field service management
b. Management Team
c. Getting Things Done
d. Vorstand

7. _____ refers to techniques, processes and tools for organizing and coordinating a group of individuals working towards a common goal--i.e. a team.

Several well-known approaches to _____ have come out of academic work. Examples include the Belbin Team Inventory by Meredith Belbin, a method to identify the different types of personalities within teams, and Ken Blanchard's description of 'High Performing Teams'.

a. 28-hour day
b. 33 Strategies of War
c. 1990 Clean Air Act
d. Team management

8. _____ is an advertisement in which a particular product specifically mentions a competitor by name for the express purpose of showing why the competitor is inferior to the product naming it.

This should not be confused with parody advertisements, where a fictional product is being advertised for the purpose of poking fun at the particular advertisement, nor should it be confused with the use of a coined brand name for the purpose of comparing the product without actually naming an actual competitor. ('Wikipedia tastes better and is less filling than the Encyclopedia Galactica.')

In the 1980s, during what has been referred to as the cola wars, soft-drink manufacturer Pepsi ran a series of advertisements where people, caught on hidden camera, in a blind taste test, chose Pepsi over rival Coca-Cola.

a. 33 Strategies of War
b. Comparative advertising
c. 1990 Clean Air Act
d. 28-hour day

9. Clayton Paul Alderfer is an American psychologist who further expanded Maslow's hierarchy of needs by categorizing the hierarchy into his _____ Alderfer categorized the lower order needs (Physiological and Safety) into the Existence category. He fit Maslow's interpersonal love and esteem needs into the relatedness category. The growth category contained the Self Actualization and self esteem needs.

Alderfer also proposed a regression theory to go along with the _____. He said that when needs in a higher category are not met then individuals redouble the efforts invested in a lower category need.

a. ERG theory
b. Abraham Harold Maslow
c. Adam Smith
d. Alvin Neill Jackson

10. _____ is the process of recruiting individuals to fill executive positions in organizations. _____ may be performed by an organization's board of directors, by executives in the organization, or by an outside _____ organization.

The _____ profession has two distinct fields, retained _____ and contingency search.

    a. Internet recruiting   b. Employment agency
    c. Executive Search   d. Employee referral

11. _____ is about the mental processes regarding choice, or choosing. It explains the processes that an individual undergoes to make choices. In organizational behavior study, _____ is a motivation theory first proposed by Victor Vroom of the Yale School of Management.

    a. A Stake in the Outcome   b. AAAI
    c. A4e   d. Expectancy theory

12. _____ refers to training in different ways to improve overall performance. It takes advantage of the particular effectiveness of each training method, while at the same time attempting to neglect the shortcomings of that method by combining it with other methods that address its weaknesses.

Cross training is employee-employer field means, training employees to do one another's work.

    a. 28-hour day   b. 1990 Clean Air Act
    c. 33 Strategies of War   d. Cross-training

13. In economics and sociology, an _____ is any factor (financial or non-financial) that enables or motivates a particular course of action, or counts as a reason for preferring one choice to the alternatives. It is an expectation that encourages people to behave in a certain way. Since human beings are purposeful creatures, the study of _____ structures is central to the study of all economic activity (both in terms of individual decision-making and in terms of co-operation and competition within a larger institutional structure.)

    a. A4e   b. A Stake in the Outcome
    c. Incentive   d. AAAI

14. _____ is the use of consequences to modify the occurrence and form of behavior. _____ is distinguished from classical conditioning (also called respondent conditioning, or Pavlovian conditioning) in that _____ deals with the modification of 'voluntary behavior' or operant behavior. Operant behavior 'operates' on the environment and is maintained by its consequences, while classical conditioning deals with the conditioning of respondent behaviors which are elicited by antecedent conditions.

    a. Unemployment insurance   b. Operant conditioning
    c. Occupational Safety and Health Administration   d. Outsourcing

15. In operant conditioning, _____ occurs when an event following a response causes an increase in the probability of that response occurring in the future. Response strength can be assessed by measures such as the frequency with which the response is made (for example, a pigeon may peck a key more times in the session), or the speed with which it is made (for example, a rat may run a maze faster.) The environment change contingent upon the response is called a reinforcer.

Chapter 14. Human Motivation

a. Diminishing Manufacturing Sources and Material Shortages
b. Historiometry
c. Meetings, Incentives, Conferences, and Exhibitions
d. Reinforcement

16. _____ attempts to explain relational satisfaction in terms of perceptions of fair/unfair distributions of resources within interpersonal relationships. _____ is considered as one of the justice theories, It was first developed in 1962 by John Stacey Adams, a workplace and behavioral psychologist, who asserted that employees seek to maintain equity between the inputs that they bring to a job and the outcomes that they receive from it against the perceived inputs and outcomes of others (Adams, 1965.) The belief is that people value fair treatment which causes them to be motivated to keep the fairness maintained within the relationships of their co-workers and the organization.

a. A Stake in the Outcome
b. A4e
c. AAAI
d. Equity theory

17. _____ describes the situation when output from (or information about the result of) an event or phenomenon in the past will influence the same event/phenomenon in the present or future. When an event is part of a chain of cause-and-effect that forms a circuit or loop, then the event is said to 'feed back' into itself.

_____ is also a synonym for:

- _____ signal; the information about the initial event that is the basis for subsequent modification of the event.
- _____ loop; the causal path that leads from the initial generation of the _____ signal to the subsequent modification of the event.

_____ is a mechanism, process or signal that is looped back to control a system within itself. Such a loop is called a _____ loop.

a. Feedback
b. 1990 Clean Air Act
c. Feedback loop
d. Positive feedback

18. _____ has become one of the most popular theories in organizational psychology.

Goal setting has been a formula used for acheivement since the early 1800s. The form and pattern has cahanged drastically over the years and there is still much debate as to what is the most efective pattern to follow.

a. Human relations
b. Goal-setting theory
c. Corporate Culture
d. Job satisfaction

19. _____ and Theory Y are theories of human motivation created and developed by Douglas McGregor at the MIT Sloan School of Management in the 1960s that have been used in human resource management, organizational behavior, organizational communication and organizational development. They describe two very different attitudes toward workforce motivation. McGregor felt that companies followed either one or the other approach.

In _____, which many managers practice, management assumes employees are inherently lazy and will avoid work if they can. They inherently dislike work. Because of this, workers need to be closely supervised and comprehensive systems of controls developed.

Chapter 14. Human Motivation

a. Management team
b. Job enrichment
c. Cash cow
d. Theory X

20. Theory X and _____ are theories of human motivation created and developed by Douglas McGregor at the MIT Sloan School of Management in the 1960s that have been used in human resource management, organizational behavior, organizational communication and organizational development. They describe two very different attitudes toward workforce motivation. McGregor felt that companies followed either one or the other approach.

In _____, management assumes employees may be ambitious and self-motivated and exercise self-control. It is believed that employees enjoy their mental and physical work duties.

a. Design leadership
b. Contingency theory
c. Business Workflow Analysis
d. Theory Y

21. In a military context, the _____ is the line of authority and responsibility along which orders are passed within a military unit and between different units. The term is also used in a civilian management context describing comparable hierarchical structures of authority.

a. Chain of command
b. French leave
c. 1990 Clean Air Act
d. 28-hour day

22. _____ is one of the managerial functions like planning, organizing, staffing and directing. It is an important function because it helps to check the errors and to take the corrective action so that deviation from standards are minimized and stated goals of the organization are achieved in desired manner. According to modern concepts, _____ is a foreseeing action whereas earlier concept of _____ was used only when errors were detected. _____ in management means setting standards, measuring actual performance and taking corrective action.

a. Decision tree pruning
b. Schedule of reinforcement
c. Turnover
d. Control

23. _____ is an organization's process of defining its strategy and making decisions on allocating its resources to pursue this strategy, including its capital and people. Various business analysis techniques can be used in _____, including SWOT analysis (Strengths, Weaknesses, Opportunities, and Threats) and PEST analysis (Political, Economic, Social, and Technological analysis) or STEER analysis involving Socio-cultural, Technological, Economic, Ecological, and Regulatory factors and EPISTEL (Environment, Political, Informatic, Social, Technological, Economic and Legal)

_____ is the formal consideration of an organization's future course. All _____ deals with at least one of three key questions:

1. 'What do we do?'
2. 'For whom do we do it?'
3. 'How do we excel?'

In business _____, the third question is better phrased 'How can we beat or avoid competition?'. (Bradford and Duncan, page 1.)

Chapter 14. Human Motivation

a. 33 Strategies of War
b. 28-hour day
c. 1990 Clean Air Act
d. Strategic planning

24. _____ is a term originating in military organization theory, but now used more commonly in business management, particularly human resource management. _____ refers to the number of subordinates a supervisor has.

In the hierarchical business organization of the past it was not uncommon to see average spans of 1 to 10 or even less. That is, one manager supervised ten employees on average.

a. Mentoring
b. Span of control
c. Senior management
d. CIFMS

25. The U.S. _____ is an independent agency of the United States government which holds primary responsibility for enforcing the federal securities laws and regulating the securities industry, the nation's stock and options exchanges, and other electronic securities markets. The SEC was created by section 4 of the Securities Exchange Act of 1934 (now codified as 15 U.S.C. Â§ 78d and commonly referred to as the 1934 Act.)

a. Securities and Exchange Commission
b. 33 Strategies of War
c. 1990 Clean Air Act
d. 28-hour day

26. An _____ is a private computer network that uses Internet technologies to securely share any part of an organization's information or operational systems with its employees. Sometimes the term refers only to the organization's internal website, but often it is a more extensive part of the organization's computer infrastructure and private websites are an important component and focal point of internal communication and collaboration.

An _____ is built from the same concepts and technologies used for the Internet, such as client-server computing and the Internet Protocol Suite (TCP/IP.)

a. AAAI
b. A Stake in the Outcome
c. Intranet
d. A4e

27. A _____ is a prediction that directly or indirectly causes itself to become true, by the very terms of the prophecy itself, due to positive feedback between belief and behavior. Although examples of such prophecies can be found in literature as far back as ancient Greece and ancient India, it is 20th-century sociologist Robert K. Merton who is credited with coining the expression '_____' and formalizing its structure and consequences. In his book Social Theory and Social Structure, Merton gives as a feature of the _____:

In other words, a prophecy declared as truth when it is actually false may sufficiently influence people, either through fear or logical confusion, so that their reactions ultimately fulfill the once-false prophecy.

a. 1990 Clean Air Act
b. Self-fulfilling prophecy
c. 33 Strategies of War
d. 28-hour day

28. The 'business case for _____', theorizes that in a global marketplace, a company that employs a diverse workforce (both men and women, people of many generations, people from ethnically and racially diverse backgrounds etc.) is better able to understand the demographics of the marketplace it serves and is thus better equipped to thrive in that marketplace than a company that has a more limited range of employee demographics.

An additional corollary suggests that a company that supports the _____ of its workforce can also improve employee satisfaction, productivity and retention.

a. Diversity
c. Trademark
b. Virtual team
d. Kanban

29. The term _____ collectively refers to all resources that determine the value and the competitiveness of an enterprise. As such, it includes as subsets the attributes that concur to building all financial statements as well as the balance sheet.

a. A4e
c. Intellectual capital
b. A Stake in the Outcome
d. AAAI

30. _____ is the science, art and technology of enclosing or protecting products for distribution, storage, sale, and use. _____ also refers to the process of design, evaluation, and production of packages. _____ can be described as a coordinated system of preparing goods for transport, warehousing, logistics, sale, and end use.

a. Supply chain management
c. Wholesalers
b. Supply chain
d. Packaging

31. _____ is an American writer on business management practices, best-known for, In Search of Excellence (co-authored with Robert H. Waterman, Jr.)

Peters was born in Baltimore, Maryland. He went to Severn School for High School and attended Cornell University, receiving a bachelor's degree in civil engineering in 1965, and a master's degree in 1966.

a. Thomas J. Peters
c. Abraham Harold Maslow
b. Affiliation
d. Adam Smith

32. Procter is a surname, and may also refer to:

- Bryan Waller Procter (pseud. Barry Cornwall), English poet
- Goodwin Procter, American law firm
- _____, consumer products multinational

a. Strict liability
c. Downstream
b. Master and Servant Acts
d. Procter ' Gamble

33. _____ is a Fortune 500, American multinational corporation headquartered in Cincinnati, Ohio, that manufactures a wide range of consumer goods. As of 2008, P'G is the 8th largest corporation in the world by market capitalization and 14th largest US company by profit.

a. Turnover
c. STAR
b. Procter ' Gamble Co.
d. Maturity of Organizations and Business Excellence - The Four-Phase Model

Chapter 14. Human Motivation

34. In neuroscience, the _____ is a collection of brain structures which attempts to regulate and control behavior by inducing pleasurable effects.

A psychological reward is a process that reinforces behavior -- something that, when offered, causes a behavior to increase in intensity. Reward is an operational concept for describing the positive value an individual ascribes to an object, behavioral act or an internal physical state.

   a. 28-hour day
   b. Reward system
   c. 1990 Clean Air Act
   d. 33 Strategies of War

35. _____ means increasing the scope of a job through extending the range of its job duties and responsibilities. This contradicts the principles of specialisation and the division of labour whereby work is divided into small units, each of which is performed repetitively by an individual worker. Some motivational theories suggest that the boredom and alienation caused by the division of labour can actually cause efficiency to fall.
   a. Centralization
   b. Delayering
   c. Mock interview
   d. Job enlargement

36. _____ is an approach to management development where an individual is moved through a schedule of assignments designed to give him or her a breadth of exposure to the entire operation.

_____ is also practiced to allow qualified employees to gain more insights into the processes of a company, and to reduce boredom and increase job satisfaction through job variation.

The term _____ can also mean the scheduled exchange of persons in offices, especially in public offices, prior to the end of incumbency or the legislative period.

   a. 28-hour day
   b. 1990 Clean Air Act
   c. 33 Strategies of War
   d. Job rotation

37. _____ is an attempt to motivate employees by giving them the opportunity to use the range of their abilities. It is an idea that was developed by the American psychologist Frederick Herzberg in the 1950s. It can be contrasted to job enlargement which simply increases the number of tasks without changing the challenge.
   a. Cash cow
   b. Job enrichment
   c. C-A-K-E
   d. Catfish effect

38. _____ is a management technique pioneered by Michael Phillips in San Francisco in the late '60's and early '70s. The concept's most visible success was by Jack Stack and his team at SRC Holdings and popularized in 1995 by John Case. The technique is to give employees all relevant financial information about the company so they can make better decisions as workers.
   a. A4e
   b. A Stake in the Outcome
   c. AAAI
   d. Open-book management

Chapter 14. Human Motivation

39. _____ is a variable work schedule, in contrast to traditional work arrangements requiring employees to work a standard 9am to 5pm day. Under _____, there is typically a core period of the day when employees are expected to be at work (for example, between 11 am and 3pm), while the rest of the working day is 'flexitime', in which employees can choose when they work, subject to achieving total daily, weekly or monthly hours in the region of what the employer expects, and subject to the necessary work being done.

A _____ policy allows staff to determine when they will work, while a flexplace policy allows staff to determine where they will work.

a. Fiduciary
c. Certificate of Incorporation
b. Bennett Amendment
d. Flextime

40. The legal _____ varies from nation to nation. The weekend is a part of the week usually lasting one or two days in which most paid workers do not work.

In Muslim-majority countries the legal work week in the Middle East is typically either Saturday through Wednesday , Saturday through Thursday or Sunday through Thursday as in Egypt.

a. Workweek
c. Business day
b. Day One Christian Ministries
d. Working Time Directive

41. _____ is an integrated communications-based process through which individuals and communities discover that existing and newly-identified needs and wants may be satisfied by the products and services of others.

_____ is defined by the American _____ Association as the activity, set of institutions, and processes for creating, communicating, delivering, and exchanging offerings that have value for customers, clients, partners, and society at large. The term developed from the original meaning which referred literally to going to market, as in shopping, or going to a market to buy or sell goods or services.

a. Disruptive technology
c. Customer relationship management
b. Marketing
d. Market development

42. _____ is a form of marketing developed from direct response marketing campaigns conducted in the 1970s and 1980s which emphasizes customer retention and satisfaction, rather than a dominant focus on point-of-sale transactions.

_____ differs from other forms of marketing in that it recognizes the long term value to the firm of keeping customers, as opposed to direct or 'Intrusion' marketing, which focuses upon acquisition of new clients by targeting majority demographics based upon prospective client lists.

_____ refers to a long-term and mutually beneficial arrangement wherein both the buyer and seller focus on value enhancement with the goal of providing a more satisfying exchange.

a. Relationship Marketing
c. 28-hour day
b. Guerrilla marketing
d. 1990 Clean Air Act

43. _____ is an idea in the field of Organizational studies and management which describes the psychology, attitudes, experiences, beliefs and Values (personal and cultural values) of an organization. It has been defined as 'the specific collection of values and norms that are shared by people and groups in an organization and that control the way they interact with each other and with stakeholders outside the organization.'

This definition continues to explain organizational values also known as 'beliefs and ideas about what kinds of goals members of an organization should pursue and ideas about the appropriate kinds or standards of behavior organizational members should use to achieve these goals. From organizational values develop organizational norms, guidelines or expectations that prescribe appropriate kinds of behavior by employees in particular situations and control the behavior of organizational members towards one another.'

_____ is not the same as corporate culture.

a. Organizational development
b. Organizational effectiveness
c. Union shop
d. Organizational culture

Chapter 15. Leadership

1. The _____ was a period in the late 18th and early 19th centuries when major changes in agriculture, manufacturing, mining, and transportation had a profound effect on the socioeconomic and cultural conditions in Britain. The changes subsequently spread throughout Europe, North America, and eventually the world. The onset of the _____ marked a major turning point in human society; almost every aspect of daily life was eventually influenced in some way.
    a. Affiliation
    b. Industrial Revolution
    c. Adam Smith
    d. Abraham Harold Maslow

2. _____ has been described as the 'process of social influence in which one person can enlist the aid and support of others in the accomplishment of a common task' . A definition more inclusive of followers comes from Alan Keith of Genentech who said '_____ is ultimately about creating a way for people to contribute to making something extraordinary happen.'

    _____ is one of the most salient aspects of the organizational context. However, defining _____ has been challenging.

    a. 1990 Clean Air Act
    b. 28-hour day
    c. Situational leadership
    d. Leadership

3. The _____ is one of the premiere professional associations for scholars dedicated to creating and disseminating knowledge about management and organizations. Founded in 1936 by two professors, the _____ is the oldest and largest scholarly management association in the world. The Academy provides a forum for university management professors and management professionals to present and publish their original research and ideas.
    a. A Stake in the Outcome
    b. Academy of Management
    c. A4e
    d. ASTD

4. Organizational culture is not the same as _____. It is wider and deeper concepts, something that an organization 'is' rather than what it 'has' (according to Buchanan and Huczynski.)

    _____ is the total sum of the values, customs, traditions and meanings that make a company unique.

    a. Job analysis
    b. Work design
    c. Path-goal theory
    d. Corporate Culture

5. In decision theory and estimation theory, the _____ of an estimator, $\hat{\theta}$, of an unknown parameter of the distribution, θ, is the expected value of the loss function

$$R(\theta, \hat{\theta}) = \mathbb{E}_\theta L(\theta, \hat{\theta}) = \int L(\theta, \hat{\theta})\, dP_\theta.$$

Chapter 15. Leadership

where dP_θ is a probability measure parametrized by θ.

- For a scalar parameter θ and a quadratic loss function,

$$L(\theta, \hat{\theta}) = (\theta - \hat{\theta})^2$$

the _____ function becomes the mean squared error of the estimate,

$$R(\theta, \hat{\theta}) = E_\theta (\theta - \hat{\theta})^2$$

- In density estimation, the unknown parameter is probability density itself. The loss function is typically chosen to be a norm in an appropriate function space. For example, for L^2 norm,

$$L(f, \hat{f}) = \|f - \hat{f}\|_2^2$$

the _____ function becomes the mean integrated squared error

$$R(f, \hat{f}) = E\|f - \hat{f}\|^2$$

a. Risk
b. Linear model
c. Risk aversion
d. Financial modeling

6. _____ is individual power based on a high level of identification with, admiration of, or respect for the powerholder.

Nationalism, Patriotism, Celebrities and well-respected people are examples of _____ in effect.

_____ is one of the Five Bases of Social Power, as defined by Bertram Raven and his colleagues[1] in 1959.

a. 1990 Clean Air Act
b. Referent power
c. 33 Strategies of War
d. 28-hour day

7. _____ is the process of recruiting individuals to fill executive positions in organizations. _____ may be performed by an organization's board of directors, by executives in the organization, or by an outside _____ organization.

The _____ profession has two distinct fields, retained _____ and contingency search.

a. Employment agency
b. Internet recruiting
c. Executive Search
d. Employee referral

Chapter 15. Leadership

8. _____ refers to increasing the spiritual, political, social or economic strength of individuals and communities. It often involves the empowered developing confidence in their own capacities.

The term Human _____ covers a vast landscape of meanings, interpretations, definitions and disciplines ranging from psychology and philosophy to the highly commercialized Self-Help industry and Motivational sciences.

   a. A4e
   b. AAAI
   c. A Stake in the Outcome
   d. Empowerment

9. The _____ captures an expanded spectrum of values and criteria for measuring organizational success: economic, ecological and social. With the ratification of the United Nations and ICLEI _____ standard for urban and community accounting in early 2007, this became the dominant approach to public sector full cost accounting. Similar UN standards apply to natural capital and human capital measurement to assist in measurements required by _____, e.g. the ecoBudget standard for reporting ecological footprint.
   a. 28-hour day
   b. 1990 Clean Air Act
   c. 33 Strategies of War
   d. Triple bottom line

10. Contingency leadership theory in organizational studies is a type of leadership theory, leadership style, and leadership model that presumes that different leadership styles are contingent to different situations. It is also referred as _____ ® theory although, as originally convened, the situational theory term is much more restrictive. The original situational theory argues that the best type of leadership is totally determined by the situational variables. Currently there are many styles of leadership.
   a. 28-hour day
   b. Situational theory
   c. Situational leadership
   d. 1990 Clean Air Act

11. _____ is an advertisement in which a particular product specifically mentions a competitor by name for the express purpose of showing why the competitor is inferior to the product naming it.

This should not be confused with parody advertisements, where a fictional product is being advertised for the purpose of poking fun at the particular advertisement, nor should it be confused with the use of a coined brand name for the purpose of comparing the product without actually naming an actual competitor. ('Wikipedia tastes better and is less filling than the Encyclopedia Galactica.')

In the 1980s, during what has been referred to as the cola wars, soft-drink manufacturer Pepsi ran a series of advertisements where people, caught on hidden camera, in a blind taste test, chose Pepsi over rival Coca-Cola.

   a. 28-hour day
   b. 33 Strategies of War
   c. 1990 Clean Air Act
   d. Comparative advertising

12. The _____ is a leadership theory in the field of organizational studies developed by Robert House in 1971 and revised in 1996. The theory that a leader's behavior is contingent to the satisfaction, motivation and performance of subordinates. The revised version also argues that the leader engage in behaviors that complement subordinate's abilities and compensate for deficiencies.

Chapter 15. Leadership

a. Sociotechnical systems
b. Corporate Culture
c. Human relations
d. Path-goal theory

13. _____ is an idea in the field of Organizational studies and management which describes the psychology, attitudes, experiences, beliefs and Values (personal and cultural values) of an organization. It has been defined as 'the specific collection of values and norms that are shared by people and groups in an organization and that control the way they interact with each other and with stakeholders outside the organization.'

This definition continues to explain organizational values also known as 'beliefs and ideas about what kinds of goals members of an organization should pursue and ideas about the appropriate kinds or standards of behavior organizational members should use to achieve these goals. From organizational values develop organizational norms, guidelines or expectations that prescribe appropriate kinds of behavior by employees in particular situations and control the behavior of organizational members towards one another.'

_____ is not the same as corporate culture.

a. Organizational effectiveness
b. Organizational development
c. Union shop
d. Organizational culture

14. _____ is an inventory strategy that strives to improve the return on investment of a business by reducing in-process inventory and its associated carrying costs. To meet _____ objectives, the process relies on signals between different points in the process. This means the process is often driven by a series of signals, or Kanban, which tell production when to make the next part. Kanban are usually 'tickets' but can be simple visual signals, such as the presence or absence of a part on a shelf. Implemented correctly, _____ can dramatically improve a manufacturing organization's return on investment, quality, and efficiency.

a. 28-hour day
b. 33 Strategies of War
c. 1990 Clean Air Act
d. Just-in-time

15. A _____ is a name or trademark connected with a product or producer. _____s have become increasingly important components of culture and the economy, now being described as 'cultural accessories and personal philosophies'.

Some people distinguish the psychological aspect of a _____ from the experiential aspect.

a. Brand loyalty
b. Brand extension
c. Brand
d. Brand awareness

16. _____ is a Japanese philosophy that focuses on continuous improvement throughout all aspects of life. When applied to the workplace, _____ activities continually improve all functions of a business, from manufacturing to management and from the CEO to the assembly line workers. By improving standardized activities and processes, _____ aims to eliminate waste.

a. Cross-docking
b. Sensitivity analysis
c. Psychological pricing
d. Kaizen

Chapter 16. Team Management and Conflict

1. _____, widely known as F. W. Taylor, was an American mechanical engineer who sought to improve industrial efficiency. He is regarded as the father of scientific management, and was one of the first management consultants.

Taylor was one of the intellectual leaders of the Efficiency Movement and his ideas, broadly conceived, were highly influential in the Progressive Era.

   a. Douglas N. Daft
   b. Frederick Winslow Taylor
   c. Jonah Jacob Goldberg
   d. Geoffrey Colvin

2. A _____ is a group of employees from various functional areas of the organization - research, engineering, marketing, finance. human resources, and operations, for example - who are all focused on a specific objective and are responsible to work as a team to improve coordination and innovation across divisions and resolve mutual problems.

   a. Graduate recruitment
   b. Sociotechnical systems
   c. Cross-functional team
   d. Goal-setting theory

3. Procter is a surname, and may also refer to:

   - Bryan Waller Procter (pseud. Barry Cornwall), English poet
   - Goodwin Procter, American law firm
   - _____, consumer products multinational

   a. Procter ' Gamble
   b. Downstream
   c. Master and Servant Acts
   d. Strict liability

4. _____ is a Fortune 500, American multinational corporation headquartered in Cincinnati, Ohio, that manufactures a wide range of consumer goods. As of 2008, P'G is the 8th largest corporation in the world by market capitalization and 14th largest US company by profit.

   a. STAR
   b. Turnover
   c. Maturity of Organizations and Business Excellence - The Four-Phase Model
   d. Procter ' Gamble Co.

5. In business and engineering, new _____ is the term used to describe the complete process of bringing a new product or service to market. There are two parallel paths involved in the NProduct development process: one involves the idea generation, product design, and detail engineering; the other involves market research and marketing analysis. Companies typically see new _____ as the first stage in generating and commercializing new products within the overall strategic process of product life cycle management used to maintain or grow their market share.

   a. Product development
   b. 1990 Clean Air Act
   c. 33 Strategies of War
   d. 28-hour day

6. The _____, 5 U.S.C. § 552a, establishes a code of fair information practices that governs the collection, maintenance, use, and dissemination of personally identifiable information about individuals that is maintained in systems of records by federal agencies. A system of records is a group of records under the control of an agency from which information is retrieved by the name of the individual or by some identifier assigned to the individual.

Chapter 16. Team Management and Conflict

a. No-FEAR Act
b. Negligence
c. Personal Responsibility and Work Opportunity Reconciliation Act
d. Privacy Act of 1974

7. _____ refers to the movement of cash into or out of a business or financial product. It is usually measured during a specified, finite period of time. Measurement of _____ can be used

- to determine a project's rate of return or value. The time of _____s into and out of projects are used as inputs in financial models such as internal rate of return, and net present value.
- to determine problems with a business's liquidity. Being profitable does not necessarily mean being liquid. A company can fail because of a shortage of cash, even while profitable.
- as an alternate measure of a business's profits when it is believed that accrual accounting concepts do not represent economic realities. For example, a company may be notionally profitable but generating little operational cash (as may be the case for a company that barters its products rather than selling for cash.) In such a case, the company may be deriving additional operating cash by issuing shares evaluating default risk, re-investment requirements, etc.

_____ is a generic term used differently depending on the context. It may be defined by users for their own purposes.

a. Gross profit
b. Sweat equity
c. Gross profit margin
d. Cash flow

8. _____ refers to planned and systematic production processes that provide confidence in a product's suitability for its intended purpose. Refer to the definition by Merriam-Webster for further information . It is a set of activities intended to ensure that products (goods and/or services) satisfy customer requirements in a systematic, reliable fashion.

a. Quality assurance
b. 28-hour day
c. 1990 Clean Air Act
d. Risk assessment

9. A _____ is a volunteer group composed of workers (or even students), usually under the leadership of their supervisor (but they can elect a team leader), who are trained to identify, analyse and solve work-related problems and present their solutions to management in order to improve the performance of the organization, and motivate and enrich the work of employees. When matured, true _____s become self-managing, having gained the confidence of management.
_____s are an alternative to the dehumanising concept of the Division of Labour, where workers or individuals are treated like robots.

a. Connectionist expert systems
b. Competency-based job descriptions
c. Certified in Production and Inventory Management
d. Quality circle

10. A _____ -- also known as a geographically dispersed team -- is a group of individuals who work across time, space, and organizational boundaries with links strengthened by webs of communication technology. They have complementary skills and are committed to a common purpose, have interdependent performance goals, and share an approach to work for which they hold themselves mutually accountable. Geographically dispersed teams allow organizations to hire and retain the best people regardless of location.

a. Kanban
b. Risk management
c. Trademark
d. Virtual team

Chapter 16. Team Management and Conflict

11. _____ consists of the processes a company uses to track and organize its contacts with its current and prospective customers. _____ software is used to support these processes; information about customers and customer interactions can be entered, stored and accessed by employees in different company departments. Typical _____ goals are to improve services provided to customers, and to use customer contact information for targeted marketing.
    a. Green marketing
    b. Marketing plan
    c. Customer relationship management
    d. Disruptive technology

12. In economics, the people in the _____ are the suppliers of labor. The _____ is all the nonmilitary people who are employed or unemployed. In 2005, the worldwide _____ was over 3 billion people.
    a. Decent work
    b. Departmentalization
    c. Pink-collar worker
    d. Labor force

13. The U.S. _____ is an independent agency of the United States government which holds primary responsibility for enforcing the federal securities laws and regulating the securities industry, the nation's stock and options exchanges, and other electronic securities markets. The SEC was created by section 4 of the Securities Exchange Act of 1934 (now codified as 15 U.S.C. Â§ 78d and commonly referred to as the 1934 Act.)
    a. 28-hour day
    b. 1990 Clean Air Act
    c. 33 Strategies of War
    d. Securities and Exchange Commission

14. _____ is the process of recruiting individuals to fill executive positions in organizations. _____ may be performed by an organization's board of directors, by executives in the organization, or by an outside _____ organization.

    The _____ profession has two distinct fields, retained _____ and contingency search.

    a. Internet recruiting
    b. Employee referral
    c. Employment agency
    d. Executive Search

15. _____ was a writer, management consultant, and self-described 'social ecologist.' Widely considered to be 'the father of modern management,' his 39 books and countless scholarly and popular articles explored how humans are organized across all sectors of society--in business, government and the nonprofit world. His writings have predicted many of the major developments of the late twentieth century, including privatization and decentralization; the rise of Japan to economic world power; the decisive importance of marketing; and the emergence of the information society with its necessity of lifelong learning. In 1959, Drucker coined the term 'knowledge worker' and later in his life considered knowledge work productivity to be the next frontier of management.
    a. Peter Ferdinand Drucker
    b. Debora L. Spar
    c. Jacques Al-Salawat Nasruddin Nasser
    d. Chrissie Hynde

16. _____ refers to increasing the spiritual, political, social or economic strength of individuals and communities. It often involves the empowered developing confidence in their own capacities.

The term Human _____ covers a vast landscape of meanings, interpretations, definitions and disciplines ranging from psychology and philosophy to the highly commercialized Self-Help industry and Motivational sciences.

Chapter 16. Team Management and Conflict

a. AAAI
b. A4e
c. A Stake in the Outcome
d. Empowerment

17. _____ has been described as the 'process of social influence in which one person can enlist the aid and support of others in the accomplishment of a common task' . A definition more inclusive of followers comes from Alan Keith of Genentech who said '_____ is ultimately about creating a way for people to contribute to making something extraordinary happen.'

_____ is one of the most salient aspects of the organizational context. However, defining _____ has been challenging.

a. Situational leadership
b. 1990 Clean Air Act
c. 28-hour day
d. Leadership

18. _____ is a method by which the job performance of an employee is evaluated _____ is a part of career development.

_____s are regular reviews of employee performance within organizations

Generally, the aims of a _____ are to:

- Give feedback on performance to employees.
- Identify employee training needs.
- Document criteria used to allocate organizational rewards.
- Form a basis for personnel decisions: salary increases, promotions, disciplinary actions, etc.
- Provide the opportunity for organizational diagnosis and development.
- Facilitate communication between employee and administraton
- Validate selection techniques and human resource policies to meet federal Equal Employment Opportunity requirements.

A common approach to assessing performance is to use a numerical or scalar rating system whereby managers are asked to score an individual against a number of objectives/attributes. In some companies, employees receive assessments from their manager, peers, subordinates and customers while also performing a self assessment.

a. Performance Appraisal
b. Progressive discipline
c. Human resource management
d. Personnel management

19. _____ is a strategic planning method used to evaluate the Strengths, Weaknesses, Opportunities, and Threats involved in a project or in a business venture. It involves specifying the objective of the business venture or project and identifying the internal and external factors that are favorable and unfavorable to achieving that objective. The technique is credited to Albert Humphrey, who led a convention at Stanford University in the 1960s and 1970s using data from Fortune 500 companies.

a. Corporate image
b. Market share
c. Marketing
d. SWOT analysis

Chapter 16. Team Management and Conflict

20. _____ is a form of communication that typically attempts to persuade potential customers to purchase or to consume more of a particular brand of product or service. 'While now central to the contemporary global economy and the reproduction of global production networks, it is only quite recently that _____ has been more than a marginal influence on patterns of sales and production. The formation of modern _____ was intimately bound up with the emergence of new forms of monopoly capitalism around the end of the 19th and beginning of the 20th century as one element in corporate strategies to create, organize and where possible control markets, especially for mass produced consumer goods.
    - a. A4e
    - b. A Stake in the Outcome
    - c. Advertising
    - d. AAAI

21. In economics, business, retail, and accounting, a _____ is the value of money that has been used up to produce something, and hence is not available for use anymore. In economics, a _____ is an alternative that is given up as a result of a decision. In business, the _____ may be one of acquisition, in which case the amount of money expended to acquire it is counted as _____.
    - a. Cost
    - b. Cost allocation
    - c. Fixed costs
    - d. Cost overrun

22. _____ is a type of thought exhibited by group members who try to minimize conflict and reach consensus without critically testing, analyzing, and evaluating ideas. Individual creativity, uniqueness, and independent thinking are lost in the pursuit of group cohesiveness, as are the advantages of reasonable balance in choice and thought that might normally be obtained by making decisions as a group. During _____, members of the group avoid promoting viewpoints outside the comfort zone of consensus thinking.
    - a. Groupthink
    - b. Self-report inventory
    - c. Diffusion of responsibility
    - d. Psychological statistics

23. In statistics and image processing, to smooth a data set is to create an approximating function that attempts to capture important patterns in the data, while leaving out noise or other fine-scale structures/rapid phenomena. Many different algorithms are used in _____. One of the most common algorithms is the 'moving average', often used to try to capture important trends in repeated statistical surveys.
    - a. 33 Strategies of War
    - b. 28-hour day
    - c. 1990 Clean Air Act
    - d. Smoothing

24. _____ is the state or fact of exclusive rights and control over property, which may be an object, land/real estate or intellectual property. An _____ right is also referred to as title. The concept of _____ has existed for thousands of years and in all cultures.
    - a. Emanation of the state
    - b. A Stake in the Outcome
    - c. A4e
    - d. Ownership

25. In economics, and cost accounting, _____ describes the total economic cost of production and is made up of variable costs, which vary according to the quantity of a good produced and include inputs such as labor and raw materials, plus fixed costs, which are independent of the quantity of a good produced and include inputs (capital) that cannot be varied in the short term, such as buildings and machinery. _____ in economics includes the total opportunity cost of each factor of production in addition to fixed and variable costs.

The rate at which _____ changes as the amount produced changes is called marginal cost.

a. 1990 Clean Air Act
b. Total Cost
c. 33 Strategies of War
d. 28-hour day

26. _____ is a financial estimate designed to help consumers and enterprise managers assess direct and indirect costs It is a form of full cost accounting.
   a. 28-hour day
   b. 1990 Clean Air Act
   c. Total Cost of Ownership
   d. 33 Strategies of War

27. _____ is a recursive process where two or more people or organizations work together in an intersection of common goals -- for example, an intellectual endeavor that is creative in nature--by sharing knowledge, learning and building consensus. _____ does not require leadership and can sometimes bring better results through decentralization and egalitarianism. In particular, teams that work collaboratively can obtain greater resources, recognition and reward when facing competition for finite resources._____ is also present in opposing goals exhibiting the notion of adversarial _____, though this is not a common case for using the term.
   a. Collectivism
   b. 1990 Clean Air Act
   c. 28-hour day
   d. Collaboration

Chapter 17. Information Management Systems

1. The _____ was a period in the late 18th and early 19th centuries when major changes in agriculture, manufacturing, mining, and transportation had a profound effect on the socioeconomic and cultural conditions in Britain. The changes subsequently spread throughout Europe, North America, and eventually the world. The onset of the _____ marked a major turning point in human society; almost every aspect of daily life was eventually influenced in some way.
   - a. Adam Smith
   - b. Abraham Harold Maslow
   - c. Affiliation
   - d. Industrial Revolution

2. An _____ is a private computer network that uses Internet technologies to securely share any part of an organization's information or operational systems with its employees. Sometimes the term refers only to the organization's internal website, but often it is a more extensive part of the organization's computer infrastructure and private websites are an important component and focal point of internal communication and collaboration.

   An _____ is built from the same concepts and technologies used for the Internet, such as client-server computing and the Internet Protocol Suite (TCP/IP.)

   - a. AAAI
   - b. A Stake in the Outcome
   - c. A4e
   - d. Intranet

3. _____ comprises a range of practices used in an organisation to identify, create, represent, distribute and enable adoption of insights and experiences. Such insights and experiences comprise knowledge, either embodied in individuals or embedded in organisational processes or practice.

   An established discipline since 1991, _____ includes courses taught in the fields of business administration, information systems, management, and library and information sciences.

   - a. 33 Strategies of War
   - b. 28-hour day
   - c. 1990 Clean Air Act
   - d. Knowledge management

4. A _____ is a list of the general tasks and responsibilities of a position. Typically, it also includes to whom the position reports, specifications such as the qualifications needed by the person in the job, salary range for the position, etc. A _____ is usually developed by conducting a job analysis, which includes examining the tasks and sequences of tasks necessary to perform the job.
   - a. Recruitment advertising
   - b. Job description
   - c. Recruitment
   - d. Recruitment Process Insourcing

5. _____ is the process of filtering for information or patterns using techniques involving collaboration among multiple agents, viewpoints, data sources, etc. Applications of _____ typically involve very large data sets. _____ methods have been applied to many different kinds of data including sensing and monitoring data - such as in mineral exploration, environmental sensing over large areas or multiple sensors; financial data - such as financial service institutions that integrate many financial sources; or in electronic commerce and web 2.0 applications where the focus is on user data, etc.
   - a. 1990 Clean Air Act
   - b. 28-hour day
   - c. 33 Strategies of War
   - d. Collaborative filtering

6. _____ is execution of a series of programs ('jobs') on a computer without human interaction.

Chapter 17. Information Management Systems

Batch jobs are set up so they can be run to completion without human interaction, so all input data is preselected through scripts or command-line parameters. This is in contrast to 'online' or interactive programs which prompt the user for such input.

- a. 1990 Clean Air Act
- b. Batch processing
- c. 33 Strategies of War
- d. 28-hour day

7. _____ consists of the mental process of thinking involved with the process of judging the merits of multiple options and selecting one of them for action. Some simple examples include deciding whether to get up in the morning or go back to sleep, or selecting a given route for a journey. More complex examples (often decisions that affect what a person thinks or their core beliefs) include choosing a lifestyle, religious affiliation, or political position.
- a. Trade study
- b. Championship mobilization
- c. Groups decision making
- d. Choice

8. _____ constitute a class of computer-based information systems including knowledge-based systems that support decision-making activities.

_____ are a specific class of computerized information systems that supports business and organizational decision-making activities. A properly-designed _____ is an interactive software-based system intended to help decision makers compile useful information from raw data, documents, personal knowledge, and/or business models to identify and solve problems and make decisions.

- a. Decision support systems
- b. 28-hour day
- c. 1990 Clean Air Act
- d. Spatial Decision Support Systems

9. _____ is an integrated communications-based process through which individuals and communities discover that existing and newly-identified needs and wants may be satisfied by the products and services of others.

_____ is defined by the American _____ Association as the activity, set of institutions, and processes for creating, communicating, delivering, and exchanging offerings that have value for customers, clients, partners, and society at large. The term developed from the original meaning which referred literally to going to market, as in shopping, or going to a market to buy or sell goods or services.

- a. Market development
- b. Disruptive technology
- c. Customer relationship management
- d. Marketing

10. _____ is a management technique pioneered by Michael Phillips in San Francisco in the late '60's and early '70s. The concept's most visible success was by Jack Stack and his team at SRC Holdings and popularized in 1995 by John Case. The technique is to give employees all relevant financial information about the company so they can make better decisions as workers.
- a. Open-book management
- b. A Stake in the Outcome
- c. AAAI
- d. A4e

11. _____ is a form of communication that typically attempts to persuade potential customers to purchase or to consume more of a particular brand of product or service. 'While now central to the contemporary global economy and the reproduction of global production networks, it is only quite recently that _____ has been more than a marginal influence on patterns of sales and production. The formation of modern _____ was intimately bound up with the emergence of new forms of monopoly capitalism around the end of the 19th and beginning of the 20th century as one element in corporate strategies to create, organize and where possible control markets, especially for mass produced consumer goods.

   a. A4e
   b. Advertising
   c. AAAI
   d. A Stake in the Outcome

12. _____ is the process of recruiting individuals to fill executive positions in organizations. _____ may be performed by an organization's board of directors, by executives in the organization, or by an outside _____ organization.

The _____ profession has two distinct fields, retained _____ and contingency search.

   a. Executive Search
   b. Employee referral
   c. Employment agency
   d. Internet recruiting

13. _____ is the intelligence of machines and the branch of computer science which aims to create it. Major _____ textbooks define the field as 'the study and design of intelligent agents,' where an intelligent agent is a system that perceives its environment and takes actions which maximize its chances of success. John McCarthy, who coined the term in 1956, defines it as 'the science and engineering of making intelligent machines.'

The field was founded on the claim that a central property of human beings, intelligence--the sapience of Homo sapiens--can be so precisely described that it can be simulated by a machine.

   a. AAAI
   b. Artificial intelligence
   c. A Stake in the Outcome
   d. A4e

14. An _____ is software that attempts to reproduce the performance of one or more human experts, most commonly in a specific problem domain, and is a traditional application and/or subfield of artificial intelligence. A wide variety of methods can be used to simulate the performance of the expert however common to most or all are 1) the creation of a so-called 'knowledgebase' which uses some knowledge representation formalism to capture the Subject Matter Experts (SME) knowledge and 2) a process of gathering that knowledge from the SME and codifying it according to the formalism, which is called knowledge engineering. _____s may or may not have learning components but a third common element is that once the system is developed it is proven by being placed in the same real world problem solving situation as the human SME, typically as an aid to human workers or a supplement to some information system.

   a. Expert system
   b. AAAI
   c. A Stake in the Outcome
   d. A4e

15. An _____ is a type of management information system intended to facilitate and support the information and decision-making needs of senior executives by providing easy access to both internal and external information relevant to meeting the strategic goals of the organization. It is commonly considered as a specialized form of a Decision Support System (DSS)

The emphasis of _____ is on graphical displays and easy-to-use user interfaces. They offer strong reporting and drill-down capabilities.

a. Executive information system
b. AAAI
c. A Stake in the Outcome
d. A4e

16. _____ is the process of estimation in unknown situations. Prediction is a similar, but more general term. Both can refer to estimation of time series, cross-sectional or longitudinal data.
   a. 33 Strategies of War
   b. 28-hour day
   c. 1990 Clean Air Act
   d. Forecasting

17. _____ is an organization's process of defining its strategy and making decisions on allocating its resources to pursue this strategy, including its capital and people. Various business analysis techniques can be used in _____, including SWOT analysis (Strengths, Weaknesses, Opportunities, and Threats) and PEST analysis (Political, Economic, Social, and Technological analysis) or STEER analysis involving Socio-cultural, Technological, Economic, Ecological, and Regulatory factors and EPISTEL (Environment, Political, Informatic, Social, Technological, Economic and Legal)

_____ is the formal consideration of an organization's future course. All _____ deals with at least one of three key questions:

1. 'What do we do?'
2. 'For whom do we do it?'
3. 'How do we excel?'

In business _____, the third question is better phrased 'How can we beat or avoid competition?'. (Bradford and Duncan, page 1.)

   a. 28-hour day
   b. 1990 Clean Air Act
   c. Strategic planning
   d. 33 Strategies of War

18. Theory X and _____ are theories of human motivation created and developed by Douglas McGregor at the MIT Sloan School of Management in the 1960s that have been used in human resource management, organizational behavior, organizational communication and organizational development. They describe two very different attitudes toward workforce motivation. McGregor felt that companies followed either one or the other approach.

In _____, management assumes employees may be ambitious and self-motivated and exercise self-control. It is believed that employees enjoy their mental and physical work duties.

   a. Contingency theory
   b. Business Workflow Analysis
   c. Theory Y
   d. Design leadership

19. The _____ is a Cabinet department of the United States government responsible for occupational safety, wage and hour standards, unemployment insurance benefits, re-employment services, and some economic statistics. Many U.S. states also have such departments. The department is headed by the United States Secretary of Labor.
   a. A4e
   b. A Stake in the Outcome
   c. AAAI
   d. United States Department of Labor

Chapter 17. Information Management Systems

20. An _____ is a person who has possession of an enterprise and assumes significant accountability for the inherent risks and the outcome. It is an ambitious leader who combines land, labor, and capital to create and market new goods or services. The term is a loanword from French and was first defined by the Irish economist Richard Cantillon.
   a. AAAI
   b. A4e
   c. A Stake in the Outcome
   d. Entrepreneur

21. _____ is subcontracting a process, such as product design or manufacturing, to a third-party company. The decision to outsource is often made in the interest of lowering cost or making better use of time and energy costs, redirecting or conserving energy directed at the competencies of a particular business, or to make more efficient use of land, labor, capital, (information) technology and resources. _____ became part of the business lexicon during the 1980s.
   a. Opinion leadership
   b. Unemployment insurance
   c. Operant conditioning
   d. Outsourcing

22. In economics, business, retail, and accounting, a _____ is the value of money that has been used up to produce something, and hence is not available for use anymore. In economics, a _____ is an alternative that is given up as a result of a decision. In business, the _____ may be one of acquisition, in which case the amount of money expended to acquire it is counted as _____.
   a. Cost overrun
   b. Fixed costs
   c. Cost allocation
   d. Cost

23. _____ is the state or fact of exclusive rights and control over property, which may be an object, land/real estate or intellectual property. An _____ right is also referred to as title. The concept of _____ has existed for thousands of years and in all cultures.
   a. A Stake in the Outcome
   b. Emanation of the state
   c. Ownership
   d. A4e

24. In economics, and cost accounting, _____ describes the total economic cost of production and is made up of variable costs, which vary according to the quantity of a good produced and include inputs such as labor and raw materials, plus fixed costs, which are independent of the quantity of a good produced and include inputs (capital) that cannot be varied in the short term, such as buildings and machinery. _____ in economics includes the total opportunity cost of each factor of production in addition to fixed and variable costs.

The rate at which _____ changes as the amount produced changes is called marginal cost.

   a. Total Cost
   b. 1990 Clean Air Act
   c. 28-hour day
   d. 33 Strategies of War

25. _____ is a financial estimate designed to help consumers and enterprise managers assess direct and indirect costs It is a form of full cost accounting.
   a. 33 Strategies of War
   b. 1990 Clean Air Act
   c. 28-hour day
   d. Total Cost of Ownership

26. _____ was a writer, management consultant, and self-described 'social ecologist.' Widely considered to be 'the father of modern management,' his 39 books and countless scholarly and popular articles explored how humans are organized across all sectors of society--in business, government and the nonprofit world. His writings have predicted many of the major developments of the late twentieth century, including privatization and decentralization; the rise of Japan to economic world power; the decisive importance of marketing; and the emergence of the information society with its necessity of lifelong learning. In 1959, Drucker coined the term 'knowledge worker' and later in his life considered knowledge work productivity to be the next frontier of management.

a. Peter Ferdinand Drucker
b. Debora L. Spar
c. Chrissie Hynde
d. Jacques Al-Salawat Nasruddin Nasser

Chapter 18. Controlling: Purpose and Process

1. _____ is a business management strategy, initially implemented by Motorola, that today enjoys widespread application in many sectors of industry.

   _____ seeks to improve the quality of process outputs by identifying and removing the causes of defects (errors) and variation in manufacturing and business processes. It uses a set of quality management methods, including statistical methods, and creates a special infrastructure of people within the organization ('Black Belts' etc.)

   a. Six Sigma
   c. Theory of constraints
   b. Takt time
   d. Production line

2. _____ is one of the managerial functions like planning, organizing, staffing and directing. It is an important function because it helps to check the errors and to take the corrective action so that deviation from standards are minimized and stated goals of the organization are achieved in desired manner. According to modern concepts, _____ is a foreseeing action whereas earlier concept of _____ was used only when errors were detected. _____ in management means setting standards, measuring actual performance and taking corrective action.

   a. Schedule of reinforcement
   c. Turnover
   b. Decision tree pruning
   d. Control

3. In game theory, an _____ is a set of moves or strategies taken by the players, or their payoffs resulting from the actions or strategies taken by all players. The two are complementary in that given knowledge of the set of strategies of all players, the final state of the game is known, as are any relevant payoffs. In a game where chance or a random event is involved, the _____ is not known from only the set of strategies, but is only realized when the random event(s) are realized.

   a. Outcome
   c. A4e
   b. A Stake in the Outcome
   d. AAAI

4. In decision theory and estimation theory, the _____ of an estimator, $\hat{\theta}$, of an unknown parameter of the distribution, θ, is the expected value of the loss function

$$R(\theta, \hat{\theta}) = \mathbb{E}_\theta L(\theta, \hat{\theta}) = \int L(\theta, \hat{\theta}) \, dP_\theta.$$

where dP_θ is a probability measure parametrized by θ.

- For a scalar parameter θ and a quadratic loss function,

$$L(\theta, \hat{\theta}) = (\theta - \hat{\theta})^2$$

the _____ function becomes the mean squared error of the estimate,

$$R(\theta, \hat{\theta}) = E_\theta (\theta - \hat{\theta})^2$$

- In density estimation, the unknown parameter is probability density itself. The loss function is typically chosen to be a norm in an appropriate function space. For example, for L^2 norm,

$$L(f, \hat{f}) = \|f - \hat{f}\|_2^2$$

the _____ function becomes the mean integrated squared error

$$R(f, \hat{f}) = E\|f - \hat{f}\|^2$$

a. Risk
b. Linear model
c. Financial modeling
d. Risk aversion

5. In economics, business, retail, and accounting, a _____ is the value of money that has been used up to produce something, and hence is not available for use anymore. In economics, a _____ is an alternative that is given up as a result of a decision. In business, the _____ may be one of acquisition, in which case the amount of money expended to acquire it is counted as _____.
   a. Fixed costs
   b. Cost overrun
   c. Cost allocation
   d. Cost

6. _____ is the state or fact of exclusive rights and control over property, which may be an object, land/real estate or intellectual property. An _____ right is also referred to as title. The concept of _____ has existed for thousands of years and in all cultures.
   a. A4e
   b. A Stake in the Outcome
   c. Emanation of the state
   d. Ownership

7. In economics, and cost accounting, _____ describes the total economic cost of production and is made up of variable costs, which vary according to the quantity of a good produced and include inputs such as labor and raw materials, plus fixed costs, which are independent of the quantity of a good produced and include inputs (capital) that cannot be varied in the short term, such as buildings and machinery. _____ in economics includes the total opportunity cost of each factor of production in addition to fixed and variable costs.

The rate at which _____ changes as the amount produced changes is called marginal cost.

a. 28-hour day
b. Total Cost
c. 1990 Clean Air Act
d. 33 Strategies of War

8. _____ is a financial estimate designed to help consumers and enterprise managers assess direct and indirect costs It is a form of full cost accounting.

a. 28-hour day
b. 33 Strategies of War
c. 1990 Clean Air Act
d. Total Cost of Ownership

9. _____ (NYSE: DE) is an American corporation based in Moline, Illinois, and the leading manufacturer of agricultural machinery in the world. In 2008, it was listed as 102nd in the Fortune 500 ranking. Deere and Company agricultural products, usually sold under the John Deere name, include tractors, combine harvesters, balers, planters/seeders, ATVs and forestry equipment.

a. 28-hour day
b. Deere ' Company
c. 33 Strategies of War
d. 1990 Clean Air Act

10. Procter is a surname, and may also refer to:

- Bryan Waller Procter (pseud. Barry Cornwall), English poet
- Goodwin Procter, American law firm
- _____, consumer products multinational

a. Strict liability
b. Procter ' Gamble
c. Downstream
d. Master and Servant Acts

11. _____ is a Fortune 500, American multinational corporation headquartered in Cincinnati, Ohio, that manufactures a wide range of consumer goods. As of 2008, P'G is the 8th largest corporation in the world by market capitalization and 14th largest US company by profit.

a. Maturity of Organizations and Business Excellence - The Four-Phase Model
b. STAR
c. Procter ' Gamble Co.
d. Turnover

12. _____ refers to metrics and measures of output from production processes, per unit of input. Labor _____, for example, is typically measured as a ratio of output per labor-hour, an input. _____ may be conceived of as a metrics of the technical or engineering efficiency of production.

a. Value engineering
b. Remanufacturing
c. Master production schedule
d. Productivity

13. _____ is understood as a business unit within the overall corporate identity which is distinguishable from other business because it serves a defined external market where management can conduct strategic planning in relation to products and markets. When companies become really large, they are best thought of as being composed of a number of businesses (or _____ s.)

Chapter 18. Controlling: Purpose and Process

In the broader domain of strategic management, the phrase '_____' came into use in the 1960s, largely as a result of General Electric's many units.

- a. Strategic drift
- b. Strategic group
- c. Switching cost
- d. Strategic business unit

14. _____ refers to planned and systematic production processes that provide confidence in a product's suitability for its intended purpose. Refer to the definition by Merriam-Webster for further information . It is a set of activities intended to ensure that products (goods and/or services) satisfy customer requirements in a systematic, reliable fashion.
- a. 28-hour day
- b. 1990 Clean Air Act
- c. Risk assessment
- d. Quality assurance

15. _____ is a business magazine published by McGraw-Hill. It was first published in 1929 (as The Business Week) under the direction of Malcolm Muir, who was serving as president of the McGraw-Hill Publishing company at the time. Its primary competitors in the national business magazine category are Fortune and Forbes, which are published bi-weekly.
- a. Democracy in America
- b. Hotel Vikas
- c. The Wealth of Nations
- d. BusinessWeek

16. _____ is a contract between two parties, one being the employer and the other being the employee. An employee may be defined as: 'A person in the service of another under any contract of hire, express or implied, oral or written, where the employer has the power or right to control and direct the employee in the material details of how the work is to be performed.' Black's Law Dictionary page 471 (5th ed. 1979.)
- a. Employment
- b. Exit interview
- c. Employment counsellor
- d. Employment rate

17. The term _____ was created by President Lyndon B. Johnson when he signed Executive Order 11246 on September 24, 1965, created to prohibit federal contractors from discriminating against employees on the basis of race, sex, creed, religion, color, or national origin. In more recent times, most employers have also added sexual orientation to the list of non-discrimination.

The Executive Order also required contractors to implement affirmative action plans to increase the participation of minorities and women in the workplace.

- a. A4e
- b. Equal Employment Opportunity
- c. AAAI
- d. A Stake in the Outcome

18. The U.S. _____ is a federal agency whose goal is ending employment discrimination. The _____ investigates discrimination complaints based on an individual's race, color, national origin, religion, sex, age, disability and retaliation for reporting and/or opposing a discriminatory practice. The Commission is also tasked with filing suits on behalf of alleged victim(s) of discrimination against employers and as an adjudicatory for claims of discrimination brought against federal agencies.
- a. Airbus SAS
- b. Airbus Industrie
- c. ARCO
- d. Equal Employment Opportunity Commission

Chapter 18. Controlling: Purpose and Process

19. _____ is the strategic and coherent approach to the management of an organisation's most valued assets - the people working there who individually and collectively contribute to the achievement of the objectives of the business. The terms '_____' and 'human resources' (HR) have largely replaced the term 'personnel management' as a description of the processes involved in managing people in organizations. In simple sense, _____ means employing people, developing their resources, utilizing, maintaining and compensating their services in tune with the job and organizational requirement.

a. Human Resource Management
b. Job knowledge
c. Progressive discipline
d. Revolving door syndrome

20. _____ describes the situation when output from (or information about the result of) an event or phenomenon in the past will influence the same event/phenomenon in the present or future. When an event is part of a chain of cause-and-effect that forms a circuit or loop, then the event is said to 'feed back' into itself.

_____ is also a synonym for:

- _____ signal; the information about the initial event that is the basis for subsequent modification of the event.
- _____ loop; the causal path that leads from the initial generation of the _____ signal to the subsequent modification of the event.

_____ is a mechanism, process or signal that is looped back to control a system within itself. Such a loop is called a _____ loop.

a. Feedback
b. Positive feedback
c. Feedback loop
d. 1990 Clean Air Act

21. _____ is an organization's process of defining its strategy and making decisions on allocating its resources to pursue this strategy, including its capital and people. Various business analysis techniques can be used in _____, including SWOT analysis (Strengths, Weaknesses, Opportunities, and Threats) and PEST analysis (Political, Economic, Social, and Technological analysis) or STEER analysis involving Socio-cultural, Technological, Economic, Ecological, and Regulatory factors and EPISTEL (Environment, Political, Informatic, Social, Technological, Economic and Legal)

_____ is the formal consideration of an organization's future course. All _____ deals with at least one of three key questions:

1. 'What do we do?'
2. 'For whom do we do it?'
3. 'How do we excel?'

In business _____, the third question is better phrased 'How can we beat or avoid competition?'. (Bradford and Duncan, page 1.)

a. 28-hour day
b. 33 Strategies of War
c. Strategic planning
d. 1990 Clean Air Act

22. _____ is a variable work schedule, in contrast to traditional work arrangements requiring employees to work a standard 9am to 5pm day. Under _____, there is typically a core period of the day when employees are expected to be at work (for example, between 11 am and 3pm), while the rest of the working day is 'flexitime', in which employees can choose when they work, subject to achieving total daily, weekly or monthly hours in the region of what the employer expects, and subject to the necessary work being done.

A _____ policy allows staff to determine when they will work, while a flexplace policy allows staff to determine where they will work.

- a. Bennett Amendment
- b. Certificate of Incorporation
- c. Fiduciary
- d. Flextime

Chapter 19. Control Techniques

1. _____ is an advertisement in which a particular product specifically mentions a competitor by name for the express purpose of showing why the competitor is inferior to the product naming it.

This should not be confused with parody advertisements, where a fictional product is being advertised for the purpose of poking fun at the particular advertisement, nor should it be confused with the use of a coined brand name for the purpose of comparing the product without actually naming an actual competitor. ('Wikipedia tastes better and is less filling than the Encyclopedia Galactica.')

In the 1980s, during what has been referred to as the cola wars, soft-drink manufacturer Pepsi ran a series of advertisements where people, caught on hidden camera, in a blind taste test, chose Pepsi over rival Coca-Cola.

   a. 28-hour day
   c. Comparative advertising
   b. 33 Strategies of War
   d. 1990 Clean Air Act

2. _____ is one of the managerial functions like planning, organizing, staffing and directing. It is an important function because it helps to check the errors and to take the corrective action so that deviation from standards are minimized and stated goals of the organization are achieved in desired manner. According to modern concepts, _____ is a foreseeing action whereas earlier concept of _____ was used only when errors were detected. _____ in management means setting standards, measuring actual performance and taking corrective action.
   a. Schedule of reinforcement
   c. Control
   b. Turnover
   d. Decision tree pruning

3. In financial accounting, a _____ or statement of financial position is a summary of a person's or organization's balances. Assets, liabilities and ownership equity are listed as of a specific date, such as the end of its financial year. A _____ is often described as a snapshot of a company's financial condition.
   a. 33 Strategies of War
   c. 28-hour day
   b. 1990 Clean Air Act
   d. Balance sheet

4. _____ is a company's financial statement that indicates how the revenue is transformed into the net income The purpose of the _____ is to show managers and investors whether the company made or lost money during the period being reported.

The important thing to remember about an _____ is that it represents a period of time.

   a. AAAI
   c. A4e
   b. A Stake in the Outcome
   d. Income statement

5. _____ refers to the movement of cash into or out of a business or financial product. It is usually measured during a specified, finite period of time. Measurement of _____ can be used

- to determine a project's rate of return or value. The time of _____s into and out of projects are used as inputs in financial models such as internal rate of return, and net present value.
- to determine problems with a business's liquidity. Being profitable does not necessarily mean being liquid. A company can fail because of a shortage of cash, even while profitable.
- as an alternate measure of a business's profits when it is believed that accrual accounting concepts do not represent economic realities. For example, a company may be notionally profitable but generating little operational cash (as may be the case for a company that barters its products rather than selling for cash.) In such a case, the company may be deriving additional operating cash by issuing shares evaluating default risk, re-investment requirements, etc.

_____ is a generic term used differently depending on the context. It may be defined by users for their own purposes.

a. Gross profit
b. Cash flow
c. Sweat equity
d. Gross profit margin

6. Procter is a surname, and may also refer to:

- Bryan Waller Procter (pseud. Barry Cornwall), English poet
- Goodwin Procter, American law firm
- _____, consumer products multinational

a. Downstream
b. Strict liability
c. Master and Servant Acts
d. Procter ' Gamble

7. _____ is a Fortune 500, American multinational corporation headquartered in Cincinnati, Ohio, that manufactures a wide range of consumer goods. As of 2008, P'G is the 8th largest corporation in the world by market capitalization and 14th largest US company by profit.

a. STAR
b. Turnover
c. Maturity of Organizations and Business Excellence - The Four-Phase Model
d. Procter ' Gamble Co.

8. _____ is a financial ratio that indicates the percentage of a company's assets are provided via debt. It is the ratio of total debt (the sum of current liabilities and long-term liabilities) and total assets (the sum of current assets, fixed assets, and other assets such as 'goodwill'.)

$$\text{Debt ratio} = \frac{\text{Total Debt}}{\text{Total Assets}}$$

or alternatively:

$$\text{Debt ratio} = \frac{\text{Total Liability}}{\text{Total Assets}}$$

Chapter 19. Control Techniques

For example, a company with $2 million in total assets and $500,000 in total liabilities would have a _____ of 25%

Like all financial ratios, a company's _____ should be compared with their industry average or other competing firms.

   a. 1990 Clean Air Act
   b. Demand forecasting
   c. Debt ratio
   d. 28-hour day

9. In finance, a _____ or accounting ratio is a ratio of two selected numerical values taken from an enterprise's financial statements. There are many standard ratios used to try to evaluate the overall financial condition of a corporation or other organization. _____s may be used by managers within a firm, by current and potential shareholders (owners) of a firm, and by a firm's creditors.
   a. Rate of return
   b. Return on sales
   c. Return on equity
   d. Financial ratio

10. Market _____ is a business, economics or investment term that refers to an asset's ability to be easily converted through an act of buying or selling without causing a significant movement in the price and with minimum loss of value. Money, or cash on hand, is the most liquid asset. An act of exchange of a less liquid asset with a more liquid asset is called liquidation.
   a. 28-hour day
   b. 1990 Clean Air Act
   c. 33 Strategies of War
   d. Liquidity

11. The general definition of an _____ is an evaluation of a person, organization, system, process, project or product. _____s are performed to ascertain the validity and reliability of information; also to provide an assessment of a system's internal control. The goal of an _____ is to express an opinion on the person / organization/system (etc) in question, under evaluation based on work done on a test basis.
   a. Internal control
   b. Audit committee
   c. A Stake in the Outcome
   d. Audit

12. _____ is the process of recruiting individuals to fill executive positions in organizations. _____ may be performed by an organization's board of directors, by executives in the organization, or by an outside _____ organization.

The _____ profession has two distinct fields, retained _____ and contingency search.

   a. Internet recruiting
   b. Employment agency
   c. Employee referral
   d. Executive Search

13. _____ generally refers to a list of all planned expenses and revenues. It is a plan for saving and spending. A _____ is an important concept in microeconomics, which uses a _____ line to illustrate the trade-offs between two or more goods.
   a. Budget
   b. 1990 Clean Air Act
   c. 33 Strategies of War
   d. 28-hour day

Chapter 19. Control Techniques

14. _____ is a technique of planning and decision-making which reverses the working process of traditional budgeting. In traditional incremental budgeting, departmental managers justify only increases over the previous year budget and what has been already spent is automatically sanctioned. No reference is made to the previous level of expenditure.
   a. 28-hour day
   b. 33 Strategies of War
   c. 1990 Clean Air Act
   d. Zero-based budgeting

15. An _____ is the annual budget of an activity stated in terms of Budget Classification Code, functional/subfunctional categories and cost accounts. It contains estimates of the total value of resources required for the performance of the operation including reimbursable work or services for others. It also includes estimates of workload in terms of total work units identified by cost accounts.
   a. Inflation rate
   b. Expected return
   c. Expected gain
   d. Operating budget

16. _____s (CAPEX or capex) are expenditures creating future benefits. A _____ is incurred when a business spends money either to buy fixed assets or to add to the value of an existing fixed asset with a useful life that extends beyond the taxable year. Capex are used by a company to acquire or upgrade physical assets such as equipment, property, or industrial buildings.
   a. Weighted average cost of capital
   b. 1990 Clean Air Act
   c. Capital expenditure
   d. Capital intensive

17. _____ consists of the processes a company uses to track and organize its contacts with its current and prospective customers. _____ software is used to support these processes; information about customers and customer interactions can be entered, stored and accessed by employees in different company departments. Typical _____ goals are to improve services provided to customers, and to use customer contact information for targeted marketing.
   a. Customer relationship management
   b. Disruptive technology
   c. Green marketing
   d. Marketing plan

18. _____ is an inventory strategy that strives to improve the return on investment of a business by reducing in-process inventory and its associated carrying costs. To meet _____ objectives, the process relies on signals between different points in the process. This means the process is often driven by a series of signals, or Kanban , which tell production when to make the next part. Kanban are usually 'tickets' but can be simple visual signals, such as the presence or absence of a part on a shelf. Implemented correctly, _____ can dramatically improve a manufacturing organization's return on investment, quality, and efficiency.
   a. 1990 Clean Air Act
   b. 33 Strategies of War
   c. 28-hour day
   d. Just-in-time

19. _____ is a habitual pattern of absence from a duty or obligation.

Frequent absence from the workplace may be indicative of poor morale or of sick building syndrome. However, many employers have implemented absence policies which make no distinction between absences for genuine illness and absence for inappropriate reasons.

   a. A Stake in the Outcome
   b. Emanation of the state
   c. A4e
   d. Absenteeism

Chapter 19. Control Techniques

20. In a human resources context, _____ or labor _____ is the rate at which an employer gains and loses employees. Simple ways to describe it are 'how long employees tend to stay' or 'the rate of traffic through the revolving door.' _____ is measured for individual companies and for their industry as a whole. If an employer is said to have a high _____ relative to its competitors, it means that employees of that company have a shorter average tenure than those of other companies in the same industry.

   a. Continuous
   b. Career portfolios
   c. Ten year occupational employment projection
   d. Turnover

21. In business and accounting, _____s are everything of value that is owned by a person or company. Any property or object of value that one possesses, usually considered as applicable to the payment of one's debts is considered an _____. Simplistically stated, _____s are things of value that can be readily converted into cash.

   a. Asset
   b. A Stake in the Outcome
   c. AAAI
   d. A4e

22. _____ is a method by which the job performance of an employee is evaluated _____ is a part of career development.

   _____s are regular reviews of employee performance within organizations

   Generally, the aims of a _____ are to:

   - Give feedback on performance to employees.
   - Identify employee training needs.
   - Document criteria used to allocate organizational rewards.
   - Form a basis for personnel decisions: salary increases, promotions, disciplinary actions, etc.
   - Provide the opportunity for organizational diagnosis and development.
   - Facilitate communication between employee and administraton
   - Validate selection techniques and human resource policies to meet federal Equal Employment Opportunity requirements.

   A common approach to assessing performance is to use a numerical or scalar rating system whereby managers are asked to score an individual against a number of objectives/attributes. In some companies, employees receive assessments from their manager, peers, subordinates and customers while also performing a self assessment.

   a. Progressive discipline
   b. Personnel management
   c. Human resource management
   d. Performance appraisal

23. In the field of human resource management, _____ is the field concerned with organizational activity aimed at bettering the performance of individuals and groups in organizational settings. It has been known by several names, including employee development, human resource development, and learning and development.

Harrison observes that the name was endlessly debated by the Chartered Institute of Personnel and Development during its review of professional standards in 1999/2000.

Chapter 19. Control Techniques

a. Person specification
b. Performance appraisal
c. Revolving door syndrome
d. Training and development

24. _____ describes the situation when output from (or information about the result of) an event or phenomenon in the past will influence the same event/phenomenon in the present or future. When an event is part of a chain of cause-and-effect that forms a circuit or loop, then the event is said to 'feed back' into itself.

_____ is also a synonym for:

- _____ signal; the information about the initial event that is the basis for subsequent modification of the event.
- _____ loop; the causal path that leads from the initial generation of the _____ signal to the subsequent modification of the event.

_____ is a mechanism, process or signal that is looped back to control a system within itself. Such a loop is called a _____ loop.

a. 1990 Clean Air Act
b. Positive feedback
c. Feedback loop
d. Feedback

25. _____ is a contract between two parties, one being the employer and the other being the employee. An employee may be defined as: 'A person in the service of another under any contract of hire, express or implied, oral or written, where the employer has the power or right to control and direct the employee in the material details of how the work is to be performed.' Black's Law Dictionary page 471 (5th ed. 1979.)

a. Exit interview
b. Employment
c. Employment rate
d. Employment counsellor

26. The term _____ was created by President Lyndon B. Johnson when he signed Executive Order 11246 on September 24, 1965, created to prohibit federal contractors from discriminating against employees on the basis of race, sex, creed, religion, color, or national origin. In more recent times, most employers have also added sexual orientation to the list of non-discrimination.

The Executive Order also required contractors to implement affirmative action plans to increase the participation of minorities and women in the workplace.

a. AAAI
b. A Stake in the Outcome
c. Equal Employment Opportunity
d. A4e

27. The U.S. _____ is a federal agency whose goal is ending employment discrimination. The _____ investigates discrimination complaints based on an individual's race, color, national origin, religion, sex, age, disability and retaliation for reporting and/or opposing a discriminatory practice. The Commission is also tasked with filing suits on behalf of alleged victim(s) of discrimination against employers and as an adjudicatory for claims of discrimination brought against federal agencies.

a. Equal Employment Opportunity Commission
b. Airbus Industrie
c. ARCO
d. Airbus SAS

Chapter 19. Control Techniques

28. _____ is a cross-disciplinary area concerned with protecting the safety, health and welfare of people engaged in work or employment. The goal of all _____ programs is to foster a work free safe environment. As a secondary effect, it may also protect co-workers, family members, employers, customers, suppliers, nearby communities, and other members of the public who are impacted by the workplace environment.
   a. AAAI
   b. A4e
   c. Occupational Safety and Health
   d. A Stake in the Outcome

29. The United States _____ is an agency of the United States Department of Labor. It was created by Congress under the Occupational Safety and Health Act, signed by President Richard M. Nixon, on December 29, 1970. Its mission is to prevent work-related injuries, illnesses, and deaths by issuing and enforcing rules (called standards) for workplace safety and health.
   a. Opinion leadership
   b. Operant conditioning
   c. Unemployment insurance
   d. Occupational Safety and Health Administration

30. In decision theory and estimation theory, the _____ of an estimator, $\hat{\theta}$, of an unknown parameter of the distribution, θ, is the expected value of the loss function

$$R(\theta, \hat{\theta}) = \mathbb{E}_\theta L(\theta, \hat{\theta}) = \int L(\theta, \hat{\theta})\, dP_\theta.$$

where dP_θ is a probability measure parametrized by θ.

- For a scalar parameter θ and a quadratic loss function,

$$L(\theta, \hat{\theta}) = (\theta - \hat{\theta})^2$$

    the _____ function becomes the mean squared error of the estimate,

$$R(\theta, \hat{\theta}) = E_\theta (\theta - \hat{\theta})^2$$

- In density estimation, the unknown parameter is probability density itself. The loss function is typically chosen to be a norm in an appropriate function space. For example, for L^2 norm,

$$L(f, \hat{f}) = \|f - \hat{f}\|_2^2$$

    the _____ function becomes the mean integrated squared error

$$R(f, \hat{f}) = E\|f - \hat{f}\|^2$$

a. Risk aversion	b. Financial modeling
c. Risk	d. Linear model

31. The _____ captures an expanded spectrum of values and criteria for measuring organizational success: economic, ecological and social. With the ratification of the United Nations and ICLEI _____ standard for urban and community accounting in early 2007, this became the dominant approach to public sector full cost accounting. Similar UN standards apply to natural capital and human capital measurement to assist in measurements required by _____, e.g. the ecoBudget standard for reporting ecological footprint.

a. 1990 Clean Air Act	b. 33 Strategies of War
c. 28-hour day	d. Triple bottom line

Chapter 20. International Management

1. _____ is an advertisement in which a particular product specifically mentions a competitor by name for the express purpose of showing why the competitor is inferior to the product naming it.

This should not be confused with parody advertisements, where a fictional product is being advertised for the purpose of poking fun at the particular advertisement, nor should it be confused with the use of a coined brand name for the purpose of comparing the product without actually naming an actual competitor. ('Wikipedia tastes better and is less filling than the Encyclopedia Galactica.')

In the 1980s, during what has been referred to as the cola wars, soft-drink manufacturer Pepsi ran a series of advertisements where people, caught on hidden camera, in a blind taste test, chose Pepsi over rival Coca-Cola.

   a. 28-hour day
   c. Comparative advertising
   b. 33 Strategies of War
   d. 1990 Clean Air Act

2. A _____ or transnational corporation is a corporation or enterprise that manages production or delivers services in more than one country. It can also be referred to as an international corporation.

The first modern _____ is generally thought to be the Dutch East India Company, established in 1602.

   a. Financial Accounting Standards Board
   c. Multinational corporation
   b. Small and medium enterprises
   d. Command center

3. _____ is the process of dispersing decision-making governance closer to the people or citizen. It includes the dispersal of administration or governance in sectors or areas like engineering, management science, political science, political economy, sociology and economics. _____ is also possible in the dispersal of population and employment.
   a. Frenemy
   c. Business plan
   b. Formula for Change
   d. Decentralization

4. _____ (NYSE: DE) is an American corporation based in Moline, Illinois, and the leading manufacturer of agricultural machinery in the world. In 2008, it was listed as 102nd in the Fortune 500 ranking. Deere and Company agricultural products, usually sold under the John Deere name, include tractors, combine harvesters, balers, planters/seeders, ATVs and forestry equipment.
   a. Deere ' Company
   c. 33 Strategies of War
   b. 1990 Clean Air Act
   d. 28-hour day

5. _____ is a type of trade policy that allows traders to act and transact without interference from government. Thus, the policy permits trading partners mutual gains from trade, with goods and services produced according to the theory of comparative advantage.

Under a _____ policy, prices are a reflection of true supply and demand, and are the sole determinant of resource allocation.

   a. 33 Strategies of War
   c. 1990 Clean Air Act
   b. 28-hour day
   d. Free Trade

Chapter 20. International Management

6. _____ is a designated group of countries that have agreed to eliminate tariffs, quotas and preferences on most (if not all) goods and services traded between them. It can be considered the second stage of economic integration. Countries choose this kind of economic integration form if their economical structures are complementary.
   - a. 28-hour day
   - b. 33 Strategies of War
   - c. 1990 Clean Air Act
   - d. Free trade area

7. The _____ is a trilateral trade bloc in North America created by the governments of the United States, Canada, and Mexico. The agreement creating the trade bloc came into force on January 1, 1994. It superseded the Canada-United States Free Trade Agreement between the U.S. and Canada.
   - a. Trade union
   - b. Business war game
   - c. Career portfolios
   - d. North American Free Trade Agreement

8. The _____, widely known as ISO, is an international-standard-setting body composed of representatives from various national standards organizations. Founded on 23 February 1947, the organization promulgates worldwide proprietary industrial and commercial standards. It is headquartered in Geneva, Switzerland.
   - a. A Stake in the Outcome
   - b. A4e
   - c. International Organization for Standardization
   - d. AAAI

9. _____ is a term used in general business practice to describe methodologies, systems, and practices designed to generate new potential business clientele, generally operated through a variety of marketing techniques. _____ facilitates a business's connection between its outgoing consumer advertising and the responses to that advertising. These processes are designed for business-to-business and direct-to-consumer strategies.
   - a. 1990 Clean Air Act
   - b. Request for Proposal
   - c. Lead generation
   - d. Lead Management

10. _____ refers to both the industry of, and the practice of, helping organizations improve their performance, primarily through the analysis of existing business problems and development of plans for improvement.

Organizations hire the services of management consultants for a number of reasons, including gaining external (and presumably objective) advice, access to the consultants' specialized expertise, or simply as extra temporary help during a one-time project, where the hiring of more permanent employees is not required.

Because of their exposure to and relationships with numerous organizations, consultancies are also said to be aware of industry 'best practices', although the transferability of such practices from one organization to another is the subject of debate.

   - a. 1990 Clean Air Act
   - b. Management Consulting
   - c. 28-hour day
   - d. 33 Strategies of War

11. _____ is understood as a business unit within the overall corporate identity which is distinguishable from other business because it serves a defined external market where management can conduct strategic planning in relation to products and markets. When companies become really large, they are best thought of as being composed of a number of businesses (or _____ s.)

In the broader domain of strategic management, the phrase '_____' came into use in the 1960s, largely as a result of General Electric's many units.

Chapter 20. International Management

a. Strategic group
c. Strategic drift
b. Switching cost
d. Strategic business unit

12. A _____ or maquila is a factory that imports materials and equipment on a duty-free and tariff-free basis for assembly or manufacturing and then re-exports the assembled product, usually back to the originating country. A maquila is also referred to as a 'twin plant', or 'in-bond' industry. Nearly half a million Mexicans are employed in _____s.

a. 1990 Clean Air Act
c. 28-hour day
b. 33 Strategies of War
d. Maquiladora

13. _____ is the process of recruiting individuals to fill executive positions in organizations. _____ may be performed by an organization's board of directors, by executives in the organization, or by an outside _____ organization.

The _____ profession has two distinct fields, retained _____ and contingency search.

a. Employee referral
c. Employment agency
b. Internet recruiting
d. Executive Search

14. _____ has been described as the 'process of social influence in which one person can enlist the aid and support of others in the accomplishment of a common task' . A definition more inclusive of followers comes from Alan Keith of Genentech who said '_____ is ultimately about creating a way for people to contribute to making something extraordinary happen.'

_____ is one of the most salient aspects of the organizational context. However, defining _____ has been challenging.

a. 28-hour day
c. Situational leadership
b. 1990 Clean Air Act
d. Leadership

15. An _____ is a person temporarily or permanently residing in a country and culture other than that of the person's upbringing or legal residence. The word comes from the Latin ex and patria (country, fatherland.)

The term is sometimes used in the context of Westerners living in non-Western countries, although it is also used to describe Westerners living in other Western countries, such as Americans living in the United Kingdom, or Britons living in Spain.

a. A Stake in the Outcome
c. Expatriate
b. AAAI
d. A4e

16. _____ is one of the managerial functions like planning, organizing, staffing and directing. It is an important function because it helps to check the errors and to take the corrective action so that deviation from standards are minimized and stated goals of the organization are achieved in desired manner.According to modern concepts, _____ is a foreseeing action whereas earlier concept of _____ was used only when errors were detected. _____ in management means setting standards, measuring actual performance and taking corrective action.

a. Decision tree pruning
c. Schedule of reinforcement
b. Control
d. Turnover

Chapter 21. Succeeding In Your Organization

1. There are two types of _____ relationships: formal and informal. Informal relationships develop on their own between partners. Formal _____, on the other hand, refers to assigned relationships, often associated with organizational _____ programs designed to promote employee development or to assist at-risk children and youth.
   - a. Real Property Administrator
   - b. Human resource management system
   - c. Fix it twice
   - d. Mentoring

2. _____ is a term defined by the Oxford English Dictionary as an individual's 'course or progress through life '. It is usually considered to pertain to remunerative work (and sometimes also formal education.)

   The etymology of the term is somewhat ironic in that it comes from the Latin word carrera, which means race .
   - a. Career planning
   - b. Career
   - c. Nursing shortage
   - d. Spatial mismatch

3. _____ is defined by Ball (1997) as:

   1. Making career choices and decisions - the traditional focus of careers interventions. The changed nature of work means that individuals may now have to revisit this process more frequently now and in the future, more than in the past.
   2. Managing the organizational career - concerns the _____ tasks of individuals within the workplace, such as decision-making, life-stage transitions, dealing with stress etc.
   3. Managing 'boundaryless' careers - refers to skills needed by workers whose employment is beyond the boundaries of a single organisation, a workstyle common among, for example, artists and designers.
   4. Taking control of one's personal development - as employers take less responsibility, employees need to take control of their own development in order to maintain and enhance their employability.

   Career planning is a subset of _____. Career planning applies the concepts of Strategic planning and Marketing to taking charge of one's professional future.
   - a. Job interview
   - b. Psychological contract
   - c. Job fair
   - d. Career management

4. _____ is a subset of career management. _____ applies the concepts of Strategic planning and Marketing to taking charge of one's professional future.
   - a. Forced retention
   - b. Military recruitment
   - c. TDY
   - d. Career planning

5. _____ is the state of being which occurs when a person, object, or service is no longer wanted even though it may still be in good working order. _____ frequently occurs because a replacement has become available that is superior in one or more aspects. Videotapes making way for DVDs

   Technical _____ may occur when a new product or technology supersedes the old, and it becomes preferred to utilize the new technology in place of the old.
   - a. Obsolescence
   - b. A4e
   - c. AAAI
   - d. A Stake in the Outcome

6. A _____ represents the mutual beliefs, perceptions, and informal obligations between an employer and an employee. It sets the dynamics for the relationship and defines the detailed practicality of the work to be done. It is distinguishable from the formal written contract of employment which, for the most part, only identifies mutual duties and responsibilities in a generalized form.

   a. Spatial mismatch
   b. Career
   c. Skilled worker
   d. Psychological contract

7. The _____ was a period in the late 18th and early 19th centuries when major changes in agriculture, manufacturing, mining, and transportation had a profound effect on the socioeconomic and cultural conditions in Britain. The changes subsequently spread throughout Europe, North America, and eventually the world. The onset of the _____ marked a major turning point in human society; almost every aspect of daily life was eventually influenced in some way.

   a. Affiliation
   b. Adam Smith
   c. Abraham Harold Maslow
   d. Industrial Revolution

8. _____, e-commuting, e-work, telework, working from home (WFH), or working at home (WAH) is a work arrangement in which employees enjoy flexibility in working location and hours. In other words, the daily commute to a central place of work is replaced by telecommunication links. Many work from home, while others, occasionally also referred to as nomad workers or web commuters utilize mobile telecommunications technology to work from coffee shops or myriad other locations.

   a. 28-hour day
   b. 1990 Clean Air Act
   c. 33 Strategies of War
   d. Telecommuting

9. The _____ Automobile Company is an automobile manufacturer based in Wolfsburg, Germany, and is the original brand within the _____ Group, as well as the largest brand by sales volume.

_____ means 'people's car' in German, in which it is pronounced . Its current tagline or slogan is Das Auto .

   a. Volkswagen
   b. Rate of return
   c. Competence-based Strategic Management
   d. Turnover

10. _____ is one of the managerial functions like planning, organizing, staffing and directing. It is an important function because it helps to check the errors and to take the corrective action so that deviation from standards are minimized and stated goals of the organization are achieved in desired manner.According to modern concepts, _____ is a foreseeing action whereas earlier concept of _____ was used only when errors were detected. _____ in management means setting standards, measuring actual performance and taking corrective action.

   a. Decision tree pruning
   b. Schedule of reinforcement
   c. Turnover
   d. Control

11. The _____ is an American federal law which allows people who are not affiliated with the government to file actions against federal contractors claiming fraud against the government. The act of filing such actions is informally called 'whistleblowing.' Persons filing under the Act stand to receive a portion (usually about 15-25 percent) of any recovered damages.

   a. False Claims Act
   b. Chrapliwy v. Uniroyal
   c. Personal Responsibility and Work Opportunity Reconciliation Act
   d. Bennett Amendment

Chapter 21. Succeeding In Your Organization

12. _____ is an American writer on business management practices, best-known for, In Search of Excellence (co-authored with Robert H. Waterman, Jr.)

Peters was born in Baltimore, Maryland. He went to Severn School for High School and attended Cornell University, receiving a bachelor's degree in civil engineering in 1965, and a master's degree in 1966.

- a. Abraham Harold Maslow
- b. Adam Smith
- c. Thomas J. Peters
- d. Affiliation

13. _____ is an area of business concerned with the production of goods and services, and involves the responsibility of ensuring that business operations are efficient in terms of using as little resource as needed, and effective in terms of meeting customer requirements. It is concerned with managing the process that converts inputs (in the forms of materials, labour and energy) into outputs (in the form of goods and services.)

Operations traditionally refers to the production of goods and services separately, although the distinction between these two main types of operations is increasingly difficult to make as manufacturers tend to merge product and service offerings.

- a. A4e
- b. Operations management
- c. A Stake in the Outcome
- d. AAAI

14. Procter is a surname, and may also refer to:

- Bryan Waller Procter (pseud. Barry Cornwall), English poet
- Goodwin Procter, American law firm
- _____, consumer products multinational

- a. Downstream
- b. Strict liability
- c. Master and Servant Acts
- d. Procter ' Gamble

15. _____ is a Fortune 500, American multinational corporation headquartered in Cincinnati, Ohio, that manufactures a wide range of consumer goods. As of 2008, P'G is the 8th largest corporation in the world by market capitalization and 14th largest US company by profit.

- a. Turnover
- b. Maturity of Organizations and Business Excellence - The Four-Phase Model
- c. STAR
- d. Procter ' Gamble Co.

16. A _____ system is a manufacturing system in which there is some amount of flexibility that allows the system to react in the case of changes, whether predicted or unpredicted. This flexibility is generally considered to fall into two categories, which both contain numerous subcategories.

The first category, machine flexibility, covers the system's ability to be changed to produce new product types, and ability to change the order of operations executed on a part. The second category is called routing flexibility, which consists of the ability to use multiple machines to perform the same operation on a part, as well as the system's ability to absorb large-scale changes, such as in volume, capacity, or capability.

a. Homeworkers
b. Manufacturing resource planning
c. Jidoka
d. Flexible manufacturing

17. The _____ of 1967, Pub. L. No. 90-202, 81 Stat. 602 (Dec. 15, 1967), codified as Chapter 14 of Title 29 of the United States Code, 29 U.S.C. Â§ 621 through 29 U.S.C. Â§ 634 (ADEA), prohibits employment discrimination against persons 40 years of age or older in the United States). The law also sets standards for pensions and benefits provided by employers and requires that information about the needs of older workers be provided to the general public.

a. Undue hardship
b. Unemployment and Farm Relief Act
c. Extra time
d. Age Discrimination in Employment Act

18. _____ is a contract between two parties, one being the employer and the other being the employee. An employee may be defined as: 'A person in the service of another under any contract of hire, express or implied, oral or written, where the employer has the power or right to control and direct the employee in the material details of how the work is to be performed.' Black's Law Dictionary page 471 (5th ed. 1979.)

a. Employment counsellor
b. Exit interview
c. Employment rate
d. Employment

19. _____ is a term applied to an organization that has created the processes, tools, and training to enable it to respond quickly to customer needs and market changes while still controlling costs and quality.

An enabling factor in becoming an agile manufacturer has been the development of manufacturing support technology that allows the marketers, the designers and the production personnel to share a common database of parts and products, to share data on production capacities and problems -- particularly where small initial problems may have larger downstream effects. It is a general proposition of manufacturing that the cost of correcting quality issues increases as the problem moves downstream, so that it is cheaper to correct quality problems at the earliest possible point in the process.

a. A4e
b. A Stake in the Outcome
c. AAAI
d. Agile manufacturing

20. _____ in engineering is a method of manufacturing in which the entire production process is controlled by computer. The traditional separated process methods are joined through a computer by CIM. This integration allows that the processes exchange information with each other and they are able to initiate actions.

a. 1990 Clean Air Act
b. 33 Strategies of War
c. Computer-integrated manufacturing
d. 28-hour day

21. _____ is the process of determining the production capacity needed by an organization to meet changing demands for its products. In the context of _____, 'capacity' is the maximum amount of work that an organization is capable of completing in a given period of time.

A discrepancy between the capacity of an organization and the demands of its customers results in inefficiency, either in under-utilized resources or unfulfilled customers.

a. Scientific management
b. Productivity
c. Remanufacturing
d. Capacity planning

22. _____ is an operational activity which does an aggregate plan for the production process, in advance of 2 to 18 months, to give an idea to management as to what quantity of materials and other resources are to be procured and when, so that the total cost of operations of the organization is kept to the minimum over that period.

The quantity of outsourcing, subcontracting of items, overtime of labor, numbers to be hired and fired in each period and the amount of inventory to be held in stock and to be backlogged for each period are decided. All of these activities are done within the framework of the company ethics, policies, and long term commitment to the society, community and the country of operation.

    a. Earned value management
    b. Aggregate planning
    c. A Stake in the Outcome
    d. Earned Schedule

23. _____ is subcontracting a process, such as product design or manufacturing, to a third-party company. The decision to outsource is often made in the interest of lowering cost or making better use of time and energy costs, redirecting or conserving energy directed at the competencies of a particular business, or to make more efficient use of land, labor, capital, (information) technology and resources. _____ became part of the business lexicon during the 1980s.

    a. Unemployment insurance
    b. Operant conditioning
    c. Outsourcing
    d. Opinion leadership

24. _____ is the level of inventory that minimizes the total inventory holding costs and ordering costs. The framework used to determine this order quantity is also known as Wilson _____ Model. The model was developed by F. W. Harris in 1913.

    a. Event management
    b. Anti-leadership
    c. Effective executive
    d. Economic order quantity

25. _____ are goods that have completed the manufacturing process but have not yet been sold or distributed to the end user.

Manufacturing has three classes of inventory:

1. Raw material
2. Work in process
3. _____

A good purchased as a 'raw material' goes into the manufacture of a product. A good only partially completed during the manufacturing process is called 'work in process'. When the good is completed as to manufacturing but not yet sold or distributed to the end-user is called a 'finished good'.

    a. 28-hour day
    b. 1990 Clean Air Act
    c. Reorder point
    d. Finished goods

26. _____ is an integrated communications-based process through which individuals and communities discover that existing and newly-identified needs and wants may be satisfied by the products and services of others.

Chapter 21. Succeeding In Your Organization

_____ is defined by the American _____ Association as the activity, set of institutions, and processes for creating, communicating, delivering, and exchanging offerings that have value for customers, clients, partners, and society at large. The term developed from the original meaning which referred literally to going to market, as in shopping, or going to a market to buy or sell goods or services.

a. Marketing
b. Market development
c. Customer relationship management
d. Disruptive technology

27. _____ is a form of marketing developed from direct response marketing campaigns conducted in the 1970s and 1980s which emphasizes customer retention and satisfaction, rather than a dominant focus on point-of-sale transactions.

_____ differs from other forms of marketing in that it recognizes the long term value to the firm of keeping customers, as opposed to direct or 'Intrusion' marketing, which focuses upon acquisition of new clients by targeting majority demographics based upon prospective client lists.

_____ refers to a long-term and mutually beneficial arrangement wherein both the buyer and seller focus on value enhancement with the goal of providing a more satisfying exchange.

a. 28-hour day
b. Guerrilla marketing
c. Relationship Marketing
d. 1990 Clean Air Act

28. The _____ is the level of inventory when a fresh order should be made with suppliers to bring the inventory up by the Economic order quantity ('EOQ'.)

The _____ for replenishment of stock occurs when the level of inventory drops down to zero. In view of instantaneous replenishment of stock the level of inventory jumps to the original level from zero level.

a. Reorder point
b. Finished goods
c. 1990 Clean Air Act
d. 28-hour day

29. _____ has been described as the 'process of social influence in which one person can enlist the aid and support of others in the accomplishment of a common task' . A definition more inclusive of followers comes from Alan Keith of Genentech who said '_____ is ultimately about creating a way for people to contribute to making something extraordinary happen.'

_____ is one of the most salient aspects of the organizational context. However, defining _____ has been challenging.

a. 28-hour day
b. 1990 Clean Air Act
c. Situational leadership
d. Leadership

Chapter 21. Succeeding In Your Organization

30. _____ is an inventory strategy that strives to improve the return on investment of a business by reducing in-process inventory and its associated carrying costs. To meet _____ objectives, the process relies on signals between different points in the process. This means the process is often driven by a series of signals, or Kanban , which tell production when to make the next part. Kanban are usually 'tickets' but can be simple visual signals, such as the presence or absence of a part on a shelf. Implemented correctly, _____ can dramatically improve a manufacturing organization's return on investment, quality, and efficiency.
   a. 33 Strategies of War
   b. Just-in-time
   c. 1990 Clean Air Act
   d. 28-hour day

31. _____ or lean production, which is often known simply as 'Lean', is a production practice that considers the expenditure of resources for any goal other than the creation of value for the end customer to be wasteful, and thus a target for elimination. Working from the perspective of the customer who consumes a product or service, 'value' is defined as any action or process that a customer would be willing to pay for. Basically, lean is centered around creating more value with less work.
   a. Theory of constraints
   b. Lean manufacturing
   c. Six Sigma
   d. Production line

32. A _____ is a type of bar chart that illustrates a project schedule. _____s illustrate the start and finish dates of the terminal elements and summary elements of a project. Terminal elements and summary elements comprise the work breakdown structure of the project.
   a. 1990 Clean Air Act
   b. 28-hour day
   c. 33 Strategies of War
   d. Gantt chart

33. The Program (or Project) Evaluation and Review Technique, commonly abbreviated _____, is a model for project management designed to analyze and represent the tasks involved in completing a given project.

    _____ is a method to analyze the involved tasks in completing a given project, specially the time needed to complete each task, and identifying the minimum time needed to complete the total project.

    _____ was developed primarily to simplify the planning and scheduling of large and complex projects.

   a. 1990 Clean Air Act
   b. 28-hour day
   c. 33 Strategies of War
   d. PERT

34. The _____, 5 U.S.C. § 552a, establishes a code of fair information practices that governs the collection, maintenance, use, and dissemination of personally identifiable information about individuals that is maintained in systems of records by federal agencies. A system of records is a group of records under the control of an agency from which information is retrieved by the name of the individual or by some identifier assigned to the individual.
   a. Personal Responsibility and Work Opportunity Reconciliation Act
   b. Privacy Act of 1974
   c. Negligence
   d. No-FEAR Act

ANSWER KEY

Chapter 1
1. d   2. d   3. c   4. d   5. a   6. d   7. d   8. d   9. d   10. b
11. b   12. b   13. d   14. c   15. d   16. a   17. a   18. c   19. d   20. b
21. d   22. c   23. a   24. b   25. d   26. d   27. b   28. c   29. d   30. d
31. c   32. d   33. c

Chapter 2
1. d   2. b   3. d   4. b   5. b   6. a   7. d   8. b   9. b   10. d
11. d   12. d   13. c   14. d   15. d   16. d   17. d   18. b   19. c   20. d
21. c   22. d   23. d   24. a   25. d   26. c   27. d   28. d   29. d   30. b
31. c   32. a   33. b   34. c   35. a   36. c   37. b   38. a   39. d   40. d
41. b   42. d   43. a   44. a   45. c   46. d   47. a   48. c   49. d   50. a
51. a   52. d   53. d   54. d   55. c

Chapter 3
1. d   2. d   3. b   4. d   5. c   6. d   7. b   8. b   9. d   10. c
11. b   12. a   13. d   14. c   15. b   16. c   17. b   18. d   19. c   20. b
21. c   22. d   23. d   24. c   25. a   26. a

Chapter 4
1. d   2. c   3. d   4. b   5. b   6. a   7. d   8. a   9. d   10. c
11. a   12. c   13. c   14. d   15. d   16. c   17. d   18. b   19. a   20. b
21. d   22. b   23. b   24. c   25. d   26. a   27. d   28. d   29. d   30. d
31. a   32. d   33. c   34. a   35. a   36. d   37. d   38. a   39. b   40. b
41. b   42. d   43. b

Chapter 5
1. d   2. c   3. a   4. d   5. c   6. d   7. d   8. c   9. d   10. a
11. d   12. d   13. b   14. d   15. a   16. a   17. c   18. a   19. d   20. d
21. b   22. c   23. d   24. a   25. a   26. d   27. d   28. d   29. d   30. a
31. b   32. b   33. c   34. b   35. d

Chapter 6
1. b   2. a   3. d   4. a   5. a   6. d   7. d   8. d   9. a   10. d
11. d   12. c   13. a   14. d   15. d   16. a   17. b   18. b   19. d   20. b
21. c   22. d   23. d

Chapter 7
1. d   2. a   3. a   4. d   5. c   6. c   7. d   8. b   9. a   10. a
11. d   12. d   13. d   14. b   15. a   16. c   17. a   18. a   19. d   20. d
21. a   22. b   23. d   24. d   25. c   26. d   27. a   28. d   29. b   30. a
31. c   32. a   33. b

ANSWER KEY

Chapter 8
1. d 2. c 3. d 4. d 5. d 6. b 7. d 8. c 9. b 10. d
11. c 12. d 13. c 14. c 15. a 16. d 17. d 18. c 19. c 20. c
21. a 22. d 23. d 24. a 25. d 26. b 27. d 28. d 29. d 30. c
31. a 32. d 33. c 34. d 35. c

Chapter 9
1. d 2. d 3. d 4. d 5. c 6. b 7. d 8. b 9. d 10. d
11. b 12. c 13. c 14. d 15. c 16. c 17. d 18. b 19. c 20. d
21. d 22. d 23. d 24. c 25. c 26. b 27. b 28. c 29. a 30. b
31. d 32. d 33. d 34. d 35. d 36. d 37. c 38. a 39. d 40. b
41. d

Chapter 10
1. d 2. d 3. c 4. d 5. b 6. c 7. d 8. b 9. c 10. d
11. a 12. a 13. a 14. d 15. d

Chapter 11
1. d 2. d 3. d 4. d 5. c 6. c 7. d 8. b 9. c 10. d
11. d 12. c 13. c 14. d 15. d 16. b 17. d 18. d 19. d 20. a
21. d 22. d 23. b 24. d 25. d 26. c 27. d 28. d 29. d 30. d
31. d 32. d 33. d 34. d 35. c 36. a 37. b 38. c 39. b 40. d
41. d 42. d

Chapter 12
1. a 2. d 3. d 4. c 5. d 6. b 7. a 8. c 9. d 10. a
11. d 12. c 13. a 14. d 15. d 16. c 17. a 18. a 19. d 20. d
21. a 22. d 23. a 24. d 25. a 26. d 27. b 28. d 29. b 30. a
31. a 32. d 33. b 34. a 35. a 36. d 37. d 38. a 39. a 40. b
41. d 42. c 43. b 44. a 45. d 46. d 47. a 48. d 49. c 50. d
51. a 52. b 53. b 54. b 55. d 56. d 57. a 58. d 59. d 60. b
61. d 62. d 63. d 64. d

Chapter 13
1. d 2. a 3. c 4. c 5. d 6. c 7. d 8. b 9. b 10. d
11. d 12. d 13. a 14. d 15. d 16. d 17. d 18. d 19. d 20. d
21. d 22. c 23. b 24. c

Chapter 14
1. d 2. d 3. d 4. d 5. d 6. b 7. d 8. b 9. a 10. c
11. d 12. d 13. c 14. b 15. d 16. d 17. a 18. b 19. d 20. d
21. a 22. d 23. d 24. b 25. a 26. c 27. b 28. a 29. c 30. d
31. a 32. d 33. b 34. b 35. d 36. d 37. b 38. d 39. d 40. a
41. b 42. a 43. d

Chapter 15
1. b	2. d	3. b	4. d	5. a	6. b	7. c	8. d	9. d	10. c
11. d	12. d	13. d	14. d	15. c	16. d				

Chapter 16
1. b	2. c	3. a	4. d	5. a	6. d	7. d	8. a	9. d	10. d
11. c	12. d	13. d	14. d	15. a	16. d	17. d	18. a	19. d	20. c
21. a	22. a	23. d	24. d	25. b	26. c	27. d			

Chapter 17
1. d	2. d	3. d	4. b	5. d	6. b	7. d	8. a	9. d	10. a
11. b	12. a	13. b	14. a	15. a	16. d	17. c	18. c	19. d	20. d
21. d	22. d	23. c	24. a	25. d	26. a				

Chapter 18
1. a	2. d	3. a	4. a	5. d	6. d	7. b	8. d	9. b	10. b
11. c	12. d	13. d	14. d	15. d	16. a	17. b	18. d	19. a	20. a
21. c	22. d								

Chapter 19
1. c	2. c	3. d	4. d	5. b	6. d	7. d	8. c	9. d	10. d
11. d	12. d	13. a	14. d	15. d	16. c	17. a	18. d	19. d	20. d
21. a	22. d	23. d	24. d	25. b	26. c	27. a	28. c	29. d	30. c
31. d									

Chapter 20
1. c	2. c	3. d	4. a	5. d	6. d	7. d	8. c	9. d	10. b
11. d	12. d	13. d	14. d	15. c	16. b				

Chapter 21
1. d	2. b	3. d	4. d	5. a	6. d	7. d	8. d	9. a	10. d
11. a	12. c	13. b	14. d	15. d	16. d	17. d	18. d	19. d	20. c
21. d	22. b	23. c	24. d	25. d	26. a	27. c	28. a	29. d	30. b
31. b	32. d	33. d	34. b						